Horizon Forbidden West Complete Guide & Walkthrough

Earlene Mante IV

Horizon Forbidden West Complete Guide & Walkthrough

Copyright © 2022 Earlene Mante IV

All rights reserved.

ISBN: 979-8-4195-0594-0

Horizon Forbidden West Complete Guide & Walkthrough

CONTENTS

1	Tips and Tricks for Beginners	4
2	Catch Up on the Lore	4
3	Pick Up and Loot Everything	4
4	You Can Craft More Ammo on the Fly	4
5	Scan Machines with the Focus	5
6	Don't Forget About Tear Damage	5
7	Campfires Are Your Friend	6
8	Sell Valuables to Get Lots of Metal Shards	6
9	Walkthrough	7
10	Reach For The Stars	7
11	The Point of the Lance	13
12	To The Brink	14
13	The Embassy	16
14	Tips and Tricks	19
15	Quick Early-Game Tips and Tricks	19
16	When traveling down slopes, Slide to travel faster!	19
17	Essential Tips and Tricks	20
18	Exploration Tips and Tricks	22
19	Combat Tips and Tricks	24
20	Things to Do First in Horizon Forbidden West	29

21	Things Horizon Forbidden West Doesn't Tell You	34
22	Best Skills	41
23	How to Get Skill Points	41
24	Skill Trees Explained	42
25	Best Skills to Get First	42
26	Passive Skill Buffs	45
27	Handy Active Skills	46
28	Must-Have Weapon Techniques	46
29	Suggested Valor Surges	47
30	How to Unlock and Use Valor Surges	48
31	How to Unlock Valor Surges	48
32	How to Use Valor Surges	48
33	How-To Guides	51
34	How to Fast Travel and Change the Time of Day	51
35	How to Destroy Red Anomalous Crystal Growths (Firegleam)	52
36	How to Override and Mount Machines	53
37	How to Get Dyes and Dye Your Outfits	54
38	How to Create Jobs and Get Upgrade Parts Quickly	55

39	How to Get and Use Face Paints	55
40	Side Quests	57
41	Deep Trouble	58
42	The Bristlebacks Part 1	61
44	The Twilight Path	63
45	Shadow from the Past	67
46	Errands	72
47	A Bigger Boom	72
48	A Dash of Courage	75
49	Collectibles	77
50	Relic Ruin Ornaments	77
51	Vista Points	87
52	Signal Lenses	88
53	Characters and Voice Actors	97
54	Aloy	97
55	Sylens	98
56	Erend	99
57	Varl	99
58	Regalla	100
59	Tilda	101
60	Additional Characters and Voice Actors	101

In Horizon 2: Forbidden West the action is presented from a third person perspective (TPP). As before, the authors give us a vast world at our disposal. On the map we can find densely overgrown terrains, frosty wastelands, sandy desert and countless ruins of the old civilization, including the remains of San Francisco. The land can be traversed on foot or on the backs of selected machines. Exploration is made easier with new tools in Aloy's toolbox and new equipment features from the first game. Focus can now point to places where the girl can climb, the Pullcaster - a rope with a hook - allows the protagonist to quickly reach high places and easily jump between platforms, while thanks to the Shieldwing - a kind of energy parachute - jumping from great heights is no longer a challenge for her. Another new feature is the ability to dive, aided by a special mask that allows Aloy to descend to great depths. These are more than 100 essential tips and tricks, strategies, and secrets you need to know to succeed in Horizon Forbidden West. Whether it's how to unlock powerful early-game weapons, how to take full advantage of the Mount system to receive free resources, or tips that make tracking down collectibles much easier, we have you covered in our comprehensive guide below.

TIPS AND TRICKS FOR BEGINNERS

If you're just about to get started with the game, this section of our Horizon Forbidden West guide is for you. Below are some Horizon Forbidden West tips and tricks that will help you out in the early goings.

Catch Up on the Lore
Horizon Forbidden West picks up the story following the events of Horizon Zero Dawn, the first game in the series. If you've played it, you should hopefully remember the complex, layered narrative that's at the very heart of these games. We would highly recommend playing through the first game before tackling Forbidden West. However, if you can't or don't want to play Zero Dawn — or maybe it's just been a while — we would recommend at least familiarising yourself with its plot. There is a lot to unpack if you're to understand Aloy's journey.

Again, there's so much that is established in that first game, and while Horizon Forbidden West does offer a very quick briefing before the game begins, it might not be quite enough, especially if you're a brand new player. The above guide should give you a far better understanding of what's happening in this fascinating setting.

Pick Up and Loot Everything
There are resources everywhere in Horizon Forbidden West, and you'll need basically all of it. This is because all the materials you find will be good for something, whether it's crafting useful traps and potions, or purchasing new gear from merchants. Even super-common resources like Medicinal Skybrush and Ridge-Wood are worth picking up if they're on the way to where you're going. In fact, those two items allow to quickly heal and craft arrows respectively, so they're arguably some of your most important pick-ups.

You should not only get into the habit of picking up stuff found naturally in the world. There are also hundreds of chests dotted around the map, and if you see one, you should definitely loot it for all it has. The same goes for any machines or humans you kill; loot their corpses for some potentially very valuable materials.

Your best friend will be a quick press of R3. Doing so will send out a "ping" from Aloy's Focus device, which will highlight items you can pick up in the surrounding area. Oh, and while Aloy does have a personal carry limit, don't worry — any surplus stuff you acquire will be automatically sent to her Stash, which you can access from any Shelter or settlement in the game. There's no excuse — pick everything up.

You Can Craft More Ammo on the Fly
Because the majority of combat is handled with projectile weapons like bows and slingshots, ammunition reserves are very important in Horizon Forbidden West — especially early on, when you can't carry very much of anything. Fortunately, you're able to craft more arrows, bombs, and bolts whenever you like, provided you have the resources necessary.

Open the weapon wheel by holding L1. Highlight the ammo you need, and then simply hold X to craft more. This goes hand-in-hand with the above tip, by the way; picking up resources frequently should mean you can craft most of your ammo without worrying about running low on materials to do so.

Scan Machines with the Focus
By holding R3 for a second, Aloy will pull up the Focus interface. While in this state, you can't move very fast, but that's not the point — the point is getting valuable information about the machines you're about to fight.

Using the right stick, you can hover the reticle over a machine, and the game will pull up a window that explains which machine you're looking at and provides a breakdown of its strengths and weaknesses. If a machine is weak to fire, for example, any fire weapons or traps you use will deal more damage against it. By the same token, if a machine is strong against fire, those same weapons will have little effect on them. Additionally, when you scan a machine, the Focus will highlight some parts of it that can either be broken off or contain useful resources.

Scanning machines is key to learning how best to deal with them, and learning about their strengths, weaknesses, and vulnerable components will often make the difference between success and defeat. Make it a habit!

Don't Forget About Tear Damage
Tear damage is a mechanic that's pretty unique to the Horizon series, and it's a very important aspect of combat you should understand. As mentioned above, using elemental weaknesses against machines puts you at a big advantage, but using ammo with Tear properties is just as useful, if not more so.

This type of damage affects a machine's component parts. Each machine in the game has lots of armour plates, weapons, and other components that can be stripped away. If a component suffers enough Tear damage, it will be removed from the machine, an act that itself usually deals a blow to the enemy's health bar.

However, there's more to it than that. If you remove armour, you will expose parts of the machine that are more vulnerable to damage, letting you land some bigger hits. If you remove a machine's weapons, you will not only strip them of one of their attacks, you will also then be able to wield that weapon against them, and those things are strong. Finally, removing certain parts from a machine can yield some of the game's most desirable resources. When you're looking to buy weapons and upgrades, or want to upgrade the ones you already have, you will often need specific components from specific machines, and these require some precision and, yes, Tear damage to acquire.

Campfires Are Your Friend
Across the expansive map of Horizon Forbidden West, you'll notice it's dotted with hundreds of Campfires. These serve a couple of very important purposes, and they shouldn't be ignored.

The game does autosave every so often, but at a Campfire, you can perform a Quick Save with the Triangle button or a Manual Save with Square — it's worth at least popping a Quick Save at any Campfire you reach. This is just to safeguard your progress; Horizon Forbidden West can be a surprisingly challenging game, and when a machine stomps you into the ground, you'll be thankful for your vigilant Campfire saves.

The second reason Campfires are great is that they not only act as fast travel points, they allow you to fast travel for free. You can fast travel from any location, but doing so requires the use of a Fast Travel Pack, which takes up resources to craft. Meanwhile, fast traveling from a Campfire doesn't cost you anything. If there's a Campfire nearby and you want to skip to another part of the map, it's worth making the short walk over and saving your materials for other things.

Sell Valuables to Get Lots of Metal Shards
Metal Shards are the main form of currency in the world of Horizon Forbidden West, and you'll need lots of them if you want to buy new equipment and items.

You will gather Metal Shards from all kinds of places — looting machines you've killed, opening treasure chests, completing missions — but you mustn't forget that you can sell stuff, too. As you play through the game, picking up everything that isn't nailed down (as you should), you will naturally accrue a collection of valuable items in Aloy's inventory.

Under the Inventory tab in the touch pad menu, scroll down to Resources. The first section is labeled 'Valuables to Sell'. These items are purely for selling to merchants and vendors, and serve no other purpose. This means these items are always safe to sell, and if you sell a bunch at once, you'll get a big boost to your Metal Shard count.

Approach most merchants in the game and you'll be able to tab over to Sell rather than Buy. Scroll down to Resources, and press Triangle on each of the items you want to sell. Once you're happy, hold X and you'll sell all the highlighted goods at once.

It's worth noting you can sell other items, like machine parts or food items, but you'll want to keep most of these things handy so you can craft stuff, make upgrades, and so on.

WALKTHROUGH

Reach For The Stars
Gather Medicinal Skybrush
Following the opening cutscene, you will need to refill your Medicine Pouch with Medicinal Skybrush Berries, which can be found growing beside the water's edge. Once you've collected one, eat it by pressing Up on the D-Pad.

While you only need to collect one, we recommend gathering enough Medical Berries (10) to fill your pouch, as these will come in handy later on in the Quest.

Go to the Ancient Ruins
Seen off in the distance, continue following the path east as it leads to a nearby waterfall. Here you have two options: you can jump down into the water or head slightly south and use the ropes to reach the ground below – it's up to you which method you take; both will see you on the ground.

From here, continue traveling east until you reach a group of Glinthawks feeding on a fallen machine. Once they flee the area, make your way down to the carcass and examine it.

Should you dive beneath the water at the base of the waterfall, you'll find a loot cache with several valuable items inside.

Gather Ridge-Wood and Craft Some Arrows

With danger potentially looming, it's time to craft some arrows. To do so, pick up some Ridge-Wood, which can be found by the edge of the water, and open the Weapon Wheel by holding L1 and crafting two Hunter Arrow packs.

With your arrows crafted, aim at the nearby ladder and shoot the red lock to lower it to the ground. Then, climb the ladder and follow the path as it leads east.

Find an Entrance to the Ancient Ruins

Now that you've reached the ancient ruins, it's time to find an entrance inside. Throughout this area, you'll discover plenty of resources and valuable loot that can later be sold for Metal Shards.

Notice all those rusted out vehicles? Scan them with your Focus to discover hidden loot, which can be accessed upon hitting it with your spear.

Ready to find the entrance, follow the path southeast, and you'll enter a short cutscene that introduces you to a new machine to the series, a Burrower. Now, you'll have two options; either it kill it with your Bow while taking advantage of its weak spot or strategically stealth past it to reach the ladder in the distance.

Should you choose stealth, simply follow a short distance behind the burrower, using the clumps of tall grass to conceal your location. Break the lock and climb up to the platform above upon reaching the ladder. Continue following the path as it leads north. At the end of the path, you'll discover the entrance to the Ancient Ruins. Before heading inside, be sure to lower the ladder along the left side of the ledge; this will create a shortcut should you wish to backtrack.

Search the Ancient Ruins for a GAIA Backup
With the ladder lowered, continue through the entrance and register as a visitor via the console at the front desk. Unable to provide access, continue through to the facility and pry open the nearby door.

Examine the Rubble in the Collapsed Wall

Having opened the door, continue up the set of stairs, and you'll discover that a large machine has destroyed a delvers camp. Wanting to gain answers, examine the rubble blocking the exit and then speak with Varl by the nearby corpse to discover an Oseram tool that Aloy can use to clear the rubble – but first, the tool will need some repairs.

After scanning the camp for potential items that can help repair the tool, examine the Satchel found inside the northernmost tent, followed by the rucksack found by the clothesline near the southeast corner of the camp. Acquiring the machine parts necessary to fix the tool, use the Workbench to craft the Pullcaster – a versatile tool that allows you to latch onto and pull grated objects, as well as grapple to specific points.

With the Pullcaster in hand, return to the rubble and wield the Pullcaster by holding L2 and then Triangle, followed by R2. Repeat this twice for both latch points to clear the rubble blocking the exit. Once removed, continue through to the next room and activate the console by Varl to watch a short hologram about the Tap to Revealfacility.

Scan the Area

After watching the Hologram display, use your Focus to scan the room to discover a grapple point on a nearby ledge, which you can reach from the rock in front of it. To grapple to a specific point, jump and tap X to attach to a grapple point.

Upon reaching the ledge, follow the path as it leads around to the ladder on the other side of the room – you'll need to grapple and climb across several gaps.

Having lowered the ladder, open the nearby door to reach the auditorium, where you'll enter a lengthy cutscene as you learn more about the history of the Tap to Reveal facility. Follow the path that leads southwest out of the auditorium and use your Pullcaster to clear the rubble blocking the way.

Once clear, continue following the path into the ruin until you enter a cutscene. Following the cutscene, wait until the Burrower walks away and then move into the next clump of Tall

Grass. Here, you'll want to equip the rock from Aloy's Hunter's Kit and proceed to throw it as far away as possible. Then, when investigating the noise, silently move from the Tall Grass and perform a Silent Strike when prompted.

With the machine taken down, continue following the path south until you reach another area infested with Burrowers. Whether you aim for their weakspots – or silent striking them as you navigate the Tall Grass – your goal will be to take down the group.

Once defeated, continue following the path east until you reach another door – head inside. Following the way through the tunnel, you'll reach an abandoned Oseram camp.

Craft Blast Traps
Before leaving the camp, let's craft some Blast Traps that you'll want for later. Requiring Machine Muscle, Blastpaste, and Metal Shards, you'll need to search the area surrounding the camp, looting any fallen machines that can be found nearby.

Once you have the required resources, select Blast Traps via Aloy's Hunter Kit and hold Down on the D-Pad to bring up the crafting menu.

With the Blast Traps crafted, head to the end of the tunnel, where you'll find a shaft that can be climbed. When reaching the top, hide in the Tall Grass and examine the Scroungers patrolling the area.

Defeat the Scroungers
Should you have crafted the Blast Traps, wait for the nearby Scrounger to move to the other side of the room and proceed to place the trap on its highlighted track in front of the Tall Grass. If you opted not to craft the traps, we recommend tagging their Power Cells as once destroyed; the Scrounger will lose the ability to shoot their laser attack.

Once the two Scroungers have been defeated, climb up to the second floor and use the handholds to make your way towards the door that's located in the eastern corner.

Open the door and climb up the set of stairs nearby, and you'll find another door – open it. However, before heading through the door, you'll find some Datapoints that can be scanned in the room east of the door.

Lower the ladder by the edge in the next room to create a shortcut back to this point. Once the ladder has been lowered, climb up the nearby handholds to reach the floor above.

Examine the Console

Continuing into the next room, examine the console found in the center, and you'll enter a lengthy cutscene that sees Aloy explaining to Varl about her origins and the task that Elisabet Sobeck has given.

Go to the Data Center
Following the cutscene, follow Varl over to the nearby door, where he'll find a Frost Blastsling

for you to use. Having obtained the weapon, continue through the door and follow the path until you reach the area outside.

Catching a glimpse of the mysterious machine responsible for killing the Oseram delvers, continue following the path spot a Scrounger - sneak up behind it, and you'll be able to take it down silently, without wasting any Blastsling Ammo or Arrows.

With the Scrounger dealt with, it's time to make your way to the top of the waterfall in the distance – you'll find plenty of ledges by the makeshift rope bridge that will allow you to climb up onto the small islands. Once you reach the top, continue forward until you reach a group of patrolling machines. First, Takedown the two Burrowers, this can be done in stealth by using the Tall Grass around the area, and once the last one is defeated, you'll also need to kill a Scrounger, who will break through a nearby wall.

Once the area is cleared, shoot down the ladder and climb up to the second floor, where you'll find another ladder on the side of the building. At the top, follow the path north into a nearby room and climb the handholds, where you'll then find yourself outside. Following a lengthy cutscene, Aloy and Varl will discover the mysterious machine was a Slitherfang, a giant snake-like machine that neither of the pair had ever seen before.

With no way to reach the Data Center without being spotted by the Slitherfang, Aloy must make her way to the space shuttle that's dangling above the Slitherfangs, with hopes of breaking it loose and crushing the dangerous machines.

Go to the Shuttle

Ready to go, rappel down to the ground below and defeat the three patrolling Burrowers. You'll want to be wary of their multiple attacks, which can include a dangerous tail swing, tossing rocks, as well as a sonic echo that will stun you for a brief moment. Do note, if you are spotted, it is best to destroy them as quickly as possible as they'll send out an alert that notifies any nearby machines of your presence.

Once the Burrowers have been defeated, continue heading east until you reach a ladder that can be shot down to reach the shuttle tower above. After climbing the ladder, look for the grapple point on a pillar above. When grappling to the point, tap Circle before reaching the point to launch up into the air – this will allow you to reach the ledge overhead. After dropping down onto the small platform, jump across to the ladder and climb to the next floor.

After looting the valuable caches around the platform, continue climbing to the top via the marked yellow ledges. When reaching the top, use your grapple to cross the gap and proceed to jump across the old rusty beams that follow. Once you've safely reached the end, use the zipline and climb the last remaining ledges once you've crossed the large gap.

Search for the Shuttle Clamp Controls

Having made it to the shuttle platform, Aloy will discover that massive clamps are holding it into place. To release these clamps, you'll need to access the Shuttle Clamp Controls console, which is found in the northeastern corner of the platform. However, before you're able to reach the console, you must defeat the Burrower and two Scroungers that patrol the area – you can take them out via stealth if you utilize the Tall Grass correctly or through good ol' combat, it's entirely up to you.

With the machines defeated, head to the control room and use the console to release the clamps, triggering a short cutscene. Unfortunately, caught up in the cables, the shuttle fails to fall, so Aloy must make the dangerous climb up the Launch Tower to manually release them herself.

Following the cutscene, head towards the Launch Tower and use the Pullcaster to remove the beam blocking the lift. With the beam removed, climb up through the hatch and follow until you reach the broken staircase.

With no way up but to climb, jump to each handhold as you make your way up to the top of the tower until you reach the first Shuttle Clamp.

Shoot the Shuttle Cable Connectors

When reaching the first Shuttle Clamp, use your Bow and Arrow to break the clamps hold on the shuttle cables.

With the first Shuttle Clamp destroyed, Aloy will need to climb higher to reach the second clamp. To do so, climb the broken set of stairs nearby and jump across the gap to the grapple point and launch yourself up into the air to reach the handhold above, and continue climbing the pillar until you reach the next platform.

From this platform, jump across the beams, and climb up the nearby ladder that leads to the second clamp. Much like the first, shoot the cable connector and watch as a cutscene unfolds. With the shuttle crashing to the ground, taking Aloy with it, she'll find herself face-to-face with a partially trapped, and understandably, very angry, Slitherfang.

Defeat the Slitherfang
With no signs of backing down, Aloy must defeat the Slitherfang if she plans on ever reaching the Data Center.

Remaining hidden behind the large boulder, take a moment to perform a scan of the giant snake-like machine, as with up to twelve unique parts, there's a lot to digest.

After cycling through all the parts and learning its weaknesses, strengths, and any key parts that you can take advantage of – including weak points, detachable containers, and parts susceptible to chain reactions – we'll want to focus the majority of our attention on the Metalbite Sac.

Slitherfang Machine Guide

Before jumping into the battle, it's important to breakdown each of the Slitherfangs attacks:

Burrowing Attack: When burrowing into the ground, continually move around the Arena without slowing down, as the Slitherfang will shoot out of the ground in your last location.

Sonic Blast: When rearing up into the air, move as quickly as possible to avoid the incoming Sonic Blasts. You'll be temporarily stunned should you get hit by one of the blasts.

Purgewater Attack: When rearing up in the air, look for clouds of white steam that appear by the Slitherfangs mouth. When this occurs, it'll mean that a Purgewater attack is incoming. The Slitherfang will shoot a blast of Purgewater across the area during this attack. If you time your dodge carefully, you'll be able to avoid taking any damage at all.

Acid Attack: Before an Acid attack is set to occur, the Slitherfang will develop a green cloud by its mouth. When it's ready to attack, it'll charge forward and sweep across the area in front of it, leaving behind clouds of Acid.

Tail Shock Attack: When coiling up and shaking its tail in the air, it'll launch its tail towards your location, slamming it into the ground, where it'll create an electrical shockwave. You'll need to quickly move out of the way and dodge this attack to avoid becoming stunned.

Charge Attack: Coiling up, the Slitherfang's eyes will begin to glow red, followed by a charging noise, before it proceeds to launch itself towards your direction, dealing large amounts of damage if you get caught. Note, this attack can destroy any obstacles blocking its path, so hiding isn't always an effective method.

Body Sweep: Rearing up into the air and leaning forward, the Slitherfang's head will move forward quickly, smashing into the ground, performing a quick body sweep that's hard to dodge, so remember to be on your toes.

Despite being relatively small and somewhat challenging to target, this acid-filled sac is frequently exposed when the Slitherfang rears up into the air. When destroyed, this part will deal devastating damage and leave the Slitherfang exposed to corrosion damage.

Using the boulders around the arena as cover, continue firing at the Slitherfang until you have destroyed the Metalbite Sac and continue killing the Slitherfang until it breaks free from the Shuttle wreckage.

Tip: In need of health or additional resources? Search the area as you'll find plenty of chests and medicinal berries nearby.

Once free of the rubble, the Slitherfang will now have access to the entire arena; however, having destroyed the Acid Sac, you'll now want to focus your attention on the Slitherfangs Data Nexus and elemental components such as the Glowblast Canister, Purgewater Canister, and Acid Canister, as you'll deal big damage when destroying these particular parts.

During the second phase, also be sure to scan the area, as you'll discover several of the Slitherfang's coil blasters have been destroyed and are now littered around the arena, ready to be picked up and used against it, these heavy weapons will give the Slitherfang a taste of its own medicine.

Head to the Data Center

Having defeated the Slitherfang, make your way to the northeast side of the arena and use the grapple point to reach the ledge above. From here, follow the path towards the door in the distance.

Search the Data Center for a GAIA Backup

Once inside the Data Center, follow the path as it leads you deeper into the center, where you'll eventually reach a door. When entering, you'll enter a lengthy cutscene that sees Aloy finally finding Tap to Reveal. With some persuasion, Aloy and Varl return to Meridian in hopes of finding Sylens and getting help to find the Tap to Reveal.

The Point of the Lance

Examine the Orb that Contained HADES

Needing to learn more about the mysterious light, examine the orb by the base of the tower that contained HADES.

Climb up to the Base of the Spire

With reasons to believe that Sylens may be responsible for the signal, it's time to climb up to the base of the Spire. To find a way up, use your Force to highlight any handholds that may help you climb onto the scaffolding. You'll find a rope at the base of the nearby crane that you can climb up and backward jump onto the scaffolding. From here, climb up the pillar and jump onto the second platform, which will allow you to use the ramp to reach the top.

Once at the top, jump onto the first crane and use your Pullcaster to pull the second crane closer.

Climb the Spire

Jump onto the second crane and use your Pullcaster once again to remove the grate located at the Spire's base. With the grate removed, proceed to climb up the tower and through the panel that is ajar. Following a cutscene, Aloy makes her way to the node at the top of the Spire, where she makes contact with Slyens.

Return to Marad and Varl

Following the events that just unfolded, speak with Marad and Varl by the large statue of Aloy.

Talk to Your Friends

Before modifying your spear, Aloy has the option to speak with her friends from the past. You'll have a chance to speak with Nasadi, Itamen, and Avad, all of which can be found by the center, not too far from the Aloy's statue. Following your conversations with Aloy's friends, head to the Workbench that's found beneath the red shade cover in the northwest corner of the area. By the workbench, you'll also find Uthid and Vanasha.

Modify Your Spear

Having spoken with your friends, it's time to modify your spear at the workbench.

Depart for The Daunt

With your spear upgrade and the area explored, speak with Marad and Varl to begin your journey west, which will conclude the Quest.

To The Brink

Go to Chainscrape

Following your conversation with Studious Vuadis, who refuses to leave the area of the lift until The Daunt has declared it safe, Aloy must head to Chainscrape to make some vital upgrades to her bow.

Before leaving the lift site, be sure to loot any nearby caches for valuables.

Following the path as it leads southwest towards the settlement, you'll encounter several Burrowers and Scroungers along the way; however, it's entirely up to you if you wish to engage with them.

Talk to the Guards and Upgrade Your Bow

When arriving at Chainscrape, speak with the guards by the entrance to gain access inside. Then, following a lengthy cutscene that sees Aloy bumping into Petra, an old ally from Zero Dawn, make your way up the ramp, and you'll find a Workbench that you use to upgrade your bow on the right, beside the Hunter Merchant.

If you wish to catch up and help complete Petra's Side Quest, speak with her inside the brewery.

Horizon Forbidden West - To The Brink UseTheWorkbench.png

Once you've upgraded your weapon via the Workbench, it's time to Find Erend.

Find Erend

With your upgraded bow, leave Chainscrape and follow the path across the river, where you'll encounter a Bristleback. Follow this machine south until you reach Erend's last known location, where you will find an Oseram Trapper perched upon an old ruin, surrounded by Scroungers.

Kill the Machines

Having riddled the area in tripwires, hide in the nearby tall grass and use rocks to lure the patrolling Scroungers into the traps to deal large amounts of damage to them and potentially stun them. Once they are stunned, launch an attack on them, preferably with Frost Damage, to take them down for good.

Alternatively, if your cover is blown, luring the Scroungers into the traps by encouraging them to chase you will also be an effective method, as you'll find several tripwires planted all around the ruin.

Having successfully taken them down, speak with the Oseram Trapper, Thurlis, to learn more about Erend's location. Before leaving, Thurlis will reward you with a Shock Tripcaster as a thank you.

Search for Erend's Tracks

Now that the Oseram Trapper is safe, scan the area with your Focus to discover Erend's tracks. With the tracks located and highlighted, follow them as they lead you further south to an old mine site, where you'll find Erend under attack from Scroungers and two Acid Bristlebacks.

Kill the Machines

With Erend moved to safety, Aloy must clear the area of machines. While you can go out gun bows-blazing, you can also take the more stealth approach that will see you using your surroundings to your advantage.

Firstly, lure the machines into the center by the machine carcass. Once the machines are grouped, shoot the clamp holding the logs suspended in the air. Upon dropping the logs, fire Acid Arrows at their Acid Canisters – preferably while they are still grouped – to cause an explosion with a chain reaction.

After defeating the machines, speak with Erend, who is nursing his badly bruised ribs, and seemly some emotional baggage relating to Aloy and how she just up and left six months ago.

Clear the Daunt

Following your conversation with Erend, it's time to clear the Daunt of machines. With an explosion nearby, head northwest and investigate the source. Upon arriving, you'll learn that the quarry is under attack by three Acid Bristlebacks – take them down. With such a large open area, your Shock Tripcaster will come in handy for this particular battle.

When attempting to take down the final Bristleback, two reinforcements will arrive – one Acid Bristleback, and one Fire Bristleback, which is weak to Shock Damage, but Fire Damage can cause an elemental explosion when targeting its Blaze Canisters.

With all Bristlebacks taken care of, loot the area and speak to the nearby Oseram Worker.

Talk to Vuadis

With the valley now deemed safe enough to travel, return to Chainscrape and speak with Vuadis, who can be found in the northern corner of the settlement, to discuss the Embassy.

Talk to Ulvund

With Ulvund refusing to leave for the Embassy until the whistle has been sounded, head to Ulvund's hut by the Campfire in Chainscrape and not so kindly persuade him to blow the whistle.

The Embassy
Override a Charger (Optional)

With the Embassy going ahead, make your way south of Chainscrape to a nearby Charger site, as you'll want to have a mount for what is about to unfold next.

Once you arrive at the machine site, hide in the tall grass at the bottom of the hill and proceed to quietly walk behind one of the machines, pressing Triangle to Override as the prompt appears.

Go to Barren Light and Speak with the Guards

Now that you have obtained a Mount, continue south until you reach the settlement known as Barren Light. When arriving, speak with the guards that are blocking the gate that leads into the Forbidden West.

Following your conversation with Lawan, follow him as he leads you to the top of the draw gate and speak with Commander Nozar. Failing to come to an agreement, Aloy will inform Nozar that she'll get through that gate, one way or another.

With Varl arriving just in time, Erend will stand up to Nozar and the guards blocking the gate will allow Aloy to pass through.

Go to the Embassy Location

With just two flags flying, follow the path forward and speak with the Tenakth Marshals at the Embassy location to find out what the hold-up is.

Following a lengthy cutscene and conversation with Marshal Fashav, he'll provide you the right of passage to travel through the Tenakth territory without any issues, should the Embassy be successful.

Just as the Embassy was about to begin, Regalla will arrive and launch an attack on the Carja and Tenakth clans. Aloy must stop Regalla's incoming Rebels, and help the Tenakth take down the unruly leader's clan.

Kill the Rebels

With Rebels attacking from all sides, it's important that you utilize cover, as the archers on the ledge and Rebels riding the Chargers will continually fire at Aloy throughout this battle.

While there are many ways to approach this fight, we recommend sticking to the center of the archway as it provides plenty of cover from the archers raining arrows down from the ledge above, while also allowing the Rebels riding Chargers just two sides to launch their attacks upon Aloy.

Although Chargers are weak to Shock Damage, should you have purchased a weapon that deals Fire Damage, we highly recommend aiming for the Chargers Blaze Canisters as it'll cause an elemental explosion.

Running short on ammunition? Listen closely during the battle and you may just hear Varl mentioning that he has drop ammo nearby.

Once you have taken down the six Chargers and Rebels, you'll face several more, along with two Bristleback riders. Much like To The Brink, aiming for the Bristlebacks Acid Canisters will cause an elemental explosion to occur, dealing large amounts of damage that will significantly aid you in this battle.

In addition to handy tips, using your Shock Tripcaster in the small stream behind the center archway will act as the perfect trap for catching the Rebels off guard, as when placed correctly, there will be a very minimal chance of them avoiding the trap.

Kill Regalla's Champion

Upon taking down two Bristlebacks, another cutscene will begin, which will see Regalla granting her Champion the honor of defeating Aloy. Jumping into battle with a nifty glider shield, Aloy must defeat the Champion if she wishes to survive.

After scanning the Rebel, you'll learn that with not only is the Champion weak to Acid and Shock Damage but also with enough damage, you'll be able to temporarily deactivate his shield.

With the Champion performing quick melee moves, you'll want to continually be moving and keeping at a distance, as you'll want to ensure you have enough time to shoot several quick attacks with your bow before he is within reaching distance, as the Champion's charge attack sees him traveling several meters very quickly.

While it's entirely up to you, we do recommend that you avoid melee attacks, as the Champion is a skilled swordsman and moves very quickly, dealing significant damage with his blade should you get caught. Furthermore, when slamming his shield into the ground, an electric shockwave will occur – it would be very difficult to dodge this attack if you are within close range.

Finally, the Champion will also occasionally throw explosive bombs and spears in Aloy's direction, which you'll want to avoid at all costs.

When moving about, try your best to flank the Champion, as when he turns his back, he'll be left exposed and susceptible to damage. After defeating Regalla's Champion, she'll grant Aloy her life as she fought an honorable battle.

Following a lengthy cutscene, the mission will end and Aloy will have access to the Shieldwing and be free to travel beyond the Daunt, into the Forbidden West.

TIPS AND TRICKS

Quick Early-Game Tips and Tricks

When starting out, pick up everything! In the early game, it's crucial to build a healthy supply of resources and materials like medicinal berries, animal parts, and machine parts, which can be used to make ammunition, traps, and even craft upgrades to your gear. Should you have these resources on hand, it will make the game's early hours easier and much more convenient, as well as reducing the need to constantly seek out these Resources as you progress through the game.

When picking up Resources, look for the list pop-up in the screen's bottom-left corner. Here, the number in brackets at the end represents your new total amount of that resource. So, for example, if a Ridgewood pickup ends in "(122)", then you now have a total of 122 Ridgewood! You're also told your pouch is full here, and those Resources have been sent to your Stash.

The Stash is an all-new feature in Forbidden West that acts as a storage chest with unlimited space. As your inventory and pouches begin to fill up, any resources collected will automatically be sent to your Stash, which can be found at all major settlements, shelters, and other specified locations around the map. For those having trouble locating their Stash, you'll commonly find it in the same area as Hunter merchants and Workbenches, so keep your eyes peeled!

When it comes to particular Settings, consider activating the Custom HUD Settings and turning Interaction Markers to Always On (found under "Player Misc"). This means the markers for Resources, Chests, and so on will always be displayed, making it much easier to tell where stuff is and if a machine/animal has something valuable.

Whether or not you have markers permanently on, it's helpful to learn their iconography. For example, triangular markers are for plants, rocks, and wood, while diamond-shaped ones are for machine parts and traps. The icon's color represents their rarity; in the case of objects with multiple items, the color reflects the object's rarest item.

Consider setting Climbing Annotations to Always On, as it isn't always obvious where the handholds are and what the best route up the surface may be. This setting will also help you reduce the need to continually ping your Focus

When traveling down slopes, Slide to travel faster!
Need Key Upgrade Resources such as Burrower Soundshells, Shellsnapper Shell Bolts, or even a Rollerback Hammer Tail? Head to Salvage Contractors to purchase unique upgrading resources at reasonable prices.

Another technique for upgrading materials is using the "Create a job" function at the Workbench. This will generate a custom quest that will automatically point you to places where you can get the parts you need for the upgrade, saving you a lot of time!

When scanning machines in the wild, any parts marked yellow will indicate you currently have a job created to obtain these items. Note, the job doesn't need the quest to be active for this to appear.

It costs 270 Shards to fully repair a Mount after reviving it from death (or 135 Shards if you've bought both of the Efficient Repair skills).

Essential Tips and Tricks
To make the most out of your time and to avoid having to backtrack to the early areas of the game, it is highly recommended that you mainline three early Main Quests - Tap to Reveal - as they unlock handy tools that are needed to explore the many hidden nooks and crannies the game has to offer. See Blocked Paths - How to Unlock All Tools

To avoid spoilers, here are the two tools you'll receive for completing the Main Quests: Tap to Reveal

On a minor note, The Embassy also unlocks the Time of Day features in Photo Mode!

At certain points throughout the game, you may need to detour and complete activities to level up and be strong enough to take on the Main Quests. Activities that give the most XP include (in descending order) Cauldrons, Tallnecks, Relic Ruins, Salvage Contracts, Rebel Camps, and Side Quests marked with green exclamation marks on the map. You can see the amount of XP an unlocked Quest or Activity will give you by going to your Quests log in the pause menu.

This same rule also applies to getting free Skill Points; the higher the XP, the more free Skill Points you'll receive.

Sides Quests and Activities unlocked further into the game will provide more XP than earlier sections. So, if you just need a quick XP boost, prioritize Quests found in the latest regions of the game you have unlocked.

The level cap in Horizon Forbidden West is 50. Once you reach it, all further Skill Points must be earned by completing quests.

Take the time to listen to rumors. Certain large establishments, such as Plainsong, will have spots where you can sit down and listen to a rumor. Much like in Ghost of Tsushima, these reveal points of interest on the map, from Cauldrons to Side Quests. So if you're at the end of the game and trying to mop up things left to do, try visiting one of these spots to find what you're missing!

While you can now Mount a wider variety of machines, be conscious of their size. Larger mounts like Bristlebacks may not fit under low arches like in Plainsong. See How to Override and Mount Machines

Despite being one of the larger mounts, the Bristleback can help you passively obtain resources. When not in use, it will begin digging into the ground, bringing up containers containing small amounts of Metal Shards.

When in stealth, avoid calling your Mount – once it nears your location, it will attract the attention of any nearby machines.

If you buy the Override Subroutines skill, you'll gain the ability to set an Overridden machine to aggressive behavior rather than defensive. They may be more trouble than it's worth, however: your Mount will follow you around and attack anything it sees, and you cannot change its behavior to defensive afterward.

After a battle, be sure to search the entire area for any potential components that may have broken off during the fight. If you were fighting on a slope, don't be surprised if some may have rolled away!

Need Metal Shards quickly to craft ammo? Navigate to your inventory and disassemble valuables and other important resources to access metal shards quickly. With that said, unless it's an emergency, you'll want to avoid disassembling too many valuables and other key items from your inventory, as selling these items via Merchants will yield you a much higher return. For example, you'll receive 20 Shards when selling an Ancient Black Bracelet to a Merchant, compared to just 10 when disassembling the item via your inventory.

Visit Cooks to purchase meals that offer temporary but powerful boosts and restore effects. With meals ranging anywhere from common to legendary, expect to find meals that boost your maximum health, increase potion proficiency and weapon stamina, along with restore effects that can increase your health and stamina by up to 75%.

Don't be surprised if you're not able to purchase items from Merchants straight away as you visit each new settlement. Instead, you'll find that Merchants will require certain animal and machine parts unique to their region in most cases.

Didn't come prepared for a challenging Quest? Don't stress, as the game provides an autosave just before starting a Quest, so if you're struggling to take down a tough Machine, don't hesitate to load into the autosave to allow yourself time to regear and adequately prepare for any upcoming battles. Boss Saves also serve the same purpose and are created just before boss fights.

When using Silent Strikes, it's important to note that it won't always kill an enemy, especially if you haven't unlocked the increased damage skills under the Infiltrator skill tree. So before going in for the kill, look for the skull icon when sneaking up on an enemy. If this skull appears, that means the stealthy attack will perform a killing blow.

To have Aloy put away her weapon at any time, bring up the Weapon Wheel and then click R3 (push the Right Analog Stick into the controller until you hear a click). Then, when you pop out of the Weapon Wheel, Aloy will put her weapon away. It even works on her spear!

When clearing certain Rebel Camps, such as Fenrise, be sure to check back in with them once you have traveled a far enough distance away. While you won't need to physically return to the settlement – checking the map will suffice – you'll notice that they'll turn into a settlement that's complete with merchants, Campfires, and Stash chests.

If you're not using Traps or other pieces of Hunter's equipment, you can remove the ones you're not using! Hold Down on the D-Pad to bring up the Hunter's Menu. From here scroll through to the item you don't want and press Square to Change. You can then press X to unequip it from your selection! This also allows you to change the order of your equipment if you need to by using empty slots.

When viewing your Inventory in the pause menu, you can press Options to change how a category is sorted. All categories can sort in Bulk or by Rarity, while some are exclusive, such as armor being sorted by their playstyle type.

Exploration Tips and Tricks
While Question Marks can represent many different things, if you're only interested in Collectibles like Vista Points, Relic Ruins, or Black Boxes, there's a clever trick to showing only them on the map. When you zoom the map all the way out with every icon turned on in the map filter, the question marks that don't vanish will always be for Collectibles!

You'll pick up Special Gear tools will allow you to clear various Blocked Path points and give you access to loot, including extremely desirable Coils and Weaves. Considering they involve zero combat, it's a good idea to scout around and clear as many of these as you can find to prepare for the battles ahead.

Don't fret about remembering where you can use the new Special Gear you unlock, as when acquiring a new tool, all Blocked Path icons on the map that require that Gear will be updated. So, for example, when you pick up the Igniter, all relevant Blocked Path icons will be updated to Firegleam icons.

When exploring the area around mission objectives, you may just find optional items that Aloy can examine, like Datapoints. While you won't miss any key story beats, these items may add additional dialogue that those invested in the story may find interesting.

After Aloy has collected the Ornament from a Relic Ruin, she'll verbally mention she should explore more if you didn't find all the loot there. When you find everything, she'll mention that too!

Forbidden West is inundated with unique dialogue moments, where characters react differently depending on whether you've met them or finished certain Quests. Unfortunately, it's practically impossible to keep track of all the permutations. Still, in general, it's a good idea to check in with your team after major events, as well as with characters who were involved with Side Quests you've completed or otherwise might know about.

Get quick and easy supplies by looking for Old Barrels scattered throughout the open world. These red rotting storage barrels can contain valuable resources.

If a chest seems out of reach, use your Focus to check if it has blue metal frameworks on it. If it does, this means that you can pull it to you with your Pullcaster!

The best spots to find Greenshine are Sunken Caverns; however, as the name implies, these can be pretty deep. To fully explore them, Tap to Reveal

Aloy's underwater breath depletes quicker the faster she swims. Therefore, swimming at top speed drains breath the fastest while staying still will barely deplete the meter. Keep this in mind if you feel the need to stop and observe your surroundings underwater.

The breathing meter, while swimming, is actually quite forgiving: when it fully depletes, you still have about ten seconds to surface for air.

If you're about to drown and would rather not lose all the items you picked up while underwater, Fast Travel! You're still able to use Fast Travel Packs while swimming, letting you zip away to safety. If you do this to The Base, it'll be for free!

While swimming, if you're using the Focus, you can still move with the left stick and use the ascend/descend controls!

While underwater, using the Focus "pulse" will send a radar pulse across the environment, revealing its topology, which can help navigate through dark spaces like sunken caves. This will also highlight points of interest, like Resource containers and walls you can Pry Open, with a pink radar ping circle.

Stumbled across a Vista Point Tower? Search the nearby area with Aloy's Focus to find the exact location of the Vista Point – in most cases, you won't need to search too far from the Tower. As you near the correct location, Aloy will begin to drop clues on where you should look.

If you're in the middle of a Vista Point hunt but need to use your Focus for its normal functions, you can press Down on the D-Pad to put the preview away. Then, press Down again to bring the preview back up.

When encountering areas covered in Blight, perform a quick scan of the environment, and you might just find fallen wildlife. Collecting these resources from fallen animals is a great and easy way to obtain wildlife resources without having to actively hunt them down.

The Shieldwing isn't just useful for gliding; it can also act as a safety parachute! Jump from a high spot, then deploy the Shieldwing shortly before hitting the ground to cushion your landing. It cuts down the time it takes to descend; however, be careful because the Shieldwing takes a moment to deploy!

Platforming sections often have ladders to kick down, walls to destroy, or pieces of the environment you can move with the Pullcaster, which are there to reduce backtracking. If you're partway through an expansive level section, remember to look out for these to avoid redoing large chunks of the level again!

Like you would see in a Far Cry game, use animal skins and other parts to upgrade your satchel and quivers carrying capacity. Although animals are much more abundant in Forbidden West, you should still take the time to scavenge them as you pass by, especially if it's an animal you don't see very often!

Rain and other weather conditions can drown out the sound of Aloy's surroundings. During these conditions, it's important that you pay extra attention to your surroundings; otherwise, you may get caught off guard.

Unless it's been mandated by the story, you can change the weather conditions by loading up a save: the weather is determined randomly whenever you do this.

When stopping by Settlements and Shelters, keep an eye out for rare and valuable caches that are often scattered throughout the camps.

Certain Old One's vehicles like cars and buses have panels that you can hit to open them, revealing boxes of loot. Use your Focus to highlight these panels in yellow!

If you're holding onto a wall handhold and the Grapple Point icon is active on screen, you only need to press X once: Aloy will jump off and automatically use the Pullcaster without the need to press X a second time!

Combat Tips and Tricks
Always have a full medicine pouch. By default, Aloy can carry ten healing berries on her, and while medicinal plants are common throughout Horizon, it can be easy to forget to stock up! So make sure you pluck some off the ground as you travel between fights.

Aloy also has a reserve pouch of medicine, displayed as a number just above the normal medicine count. You can quickly top up your medicine using your reserve pouch by holding Up on the D-Pad.

If you can, Scan with the Focus before engaging in a proper fight. This allows you to locate and tag any machines, pin any components you may want to remove, see their scouting paths, and more. As you'll quickly learn, it's always better to go in prepared!

Pre-existing machine corpses can still be used! In addition to salvaging them for resources like proper kills, certain machines like Bellowbacks will still have parts you can hit for explosive effects, essentially making them free traps.

Use Aloy's Dodge movement to create a moment of invincibility. Do note the Dodge move doesn't need pinpoint timing; just dodging away, in general, is enough to prevent Aloy from getting hit by an attack when it's close enough to hit her.

At the start of a machine fight, you should use weapons and ammo with High Tear damage and use them to destroy a machine's components. A large chunk of health is taken off whenever you do this, and certain parts will also disable specific attacks and functions. You can highlight components by scanning a machine with the Focus, but memorizing them will, of course, be faster. You can tear components off even faster with our favorite Valor Surge, Part Breaker.

Once you've exhausted all components (or at least the easier ones to hit), switch to weapons and ammo with High Impact damage to take off more health when hitting a machine in general. This is a handy tactic if a machine has small, protected, or hard-to-hit components, like the Sunwing.

On that topic, if a machine has large sacs of elemental material, like those on a Spikesnout or Bellowback, aim for them! They will often cause an enormous elemental explosion that will damage everything in a wide radius, including the target!

Some machines have components that will only explode when hit with specific elemental ammo. For example, Blaze Canisters like those on a Fanghorn will violently explode if you hit them with fire-based ammo.

Try grouping up machines with the same type of canisters – this is best done using rocks before a fight – as once they are close together, shooting a canister will see it explode. This will cause a chain reaction to ignite and explode other machine canisters.

Be careful to avoid areas in which machines deploy their radars. This behavior allows machines to temporarily disable your Focus while also detecting your location, even if you happen to be hidden from their sight.

Dispose of Scrounger and Scrapper machines quickly! While they may appear harmless when salvaging machine carcasses, the longer they scavenge, the more likely they'll steal valuable resources.

Before traveling into the Forbidden West, stop by the Hunting Goods merchant and purchase a Fire Hunter Bow; it'll come in handy for tackling some of the more powerful machines beyond The Daunt, which are weak against the fire element. With that said, you'll want to make it a goal to eventually have access to weapons of all elemental types, as machines can be weak or immune to a wide variety of elements.

Need a particular component from a machine? Make sure to target and break off the attached component before killing it; otherwise, the external component will be destroyed upon the machine's death.

This doesn't apply if you're playing on Story or Easy difficulty; however, in that case, the components can be looted from the machine after downing it.

When attempting to remove a component, be sure to use a weapon or ammo that inflicts Tear damage. This will make tearing off components much easier.

If you're in need of a heavy weapon but couldn't shoot one off of one you just killed, don't fret! You can still shoot the weapon off the machine carcass and grab it that way.

Tired of machines calling for reinforcements? Destroy or detach their antennas to prevent them from communicating with other machines.

Be careful when hiding in locations that are scanned by Recon machine types. Equipped with unique sensors and a Radar ability that disables your Focus and detects your location, these machines are designed solely to seek out intruders and keep a watchful eye over other machines and specific locations.

If you need to study the strengths and weaknesses of a particular machine, open up the Machine Catalogue via the Notebook in the pause menu, to find everything you need to know about a machine. Whether it's their loot percentages, weaknesses, or Cauldron you need to visit to learn their Override, this handy Notebook has you covered.

Since human opponents have no components, Tear Ammo isn't as effective. Therefore, you should use other arrow types that deal more impact damage instead.

Tired of running out of supplies to craft ammunition? Unlock the passive boost, Ammo Expert, under the Hunter Skill Tree, which will allow you to craft more ammunition from the same amount of resources. This skill can be upgraded twice, with the second upgrade providing a moderate increase in the amount you can craft in each set. See more Best Skills

After a battle with machines, you can easily identify any knocked-off components by their bright blue sparks. Very handy if you don't like having item markers on at all times.

If you're performing a melee combo that requires a pause in the middle, look for the glint that appears on the spear (you'll also hear a sheen sound from your TV and controller). Then, hit the next button input right on this glint to successfully continue the combo.

If one or more enemies are suspicious of you (or in the "yellow state"), a yellow icon with a ? appears at the top of the screen. If you've lost them, a white ring will appear around the icon as they search for you: when this ring depletes, the enemies will give up and return to normal.

There are no penalties for switching between difficulties in Horizon Forbidden West. So, if you're looking for quick and easy machine parts, consider lowering your difficulty level to Story or Easy. Not only will you take down machines much quicker, but machine parts won't disappear if you don't detach them first, unlike higher difficulties, which see machine parts destroyed if they weren't broken off.

Don't sleep on coils, especially those that offer a percentage chance of dealing instant elemental damage. So, if you're running a weapon that focuses mainly on Impact, Tear, and Explosive Damage, pair the weapon with elemental-based coils to get the best of both worlds.

Be aware of arrow drop when aiming. Despite not having a throwing arc, like Blastslings, arrows fired from bows do suffer from gravity over a distance. When aiming at your targets, you'll want to keep this in mind, especially over long distances with Hunter and Sharpshot Bows.

Prioritize when and where you use ammo types. More advanced ammo costs more resources to craft, and you can't hold as many of them, so you'll only want to use them when the situation demands it. For example, if your bow can fire normal arrows and Advanced Hunting Arrows, make sure you're not using the latter if you're only going to be shooting wildlife.

Deploy the Shieldwing to break your fall and land cleanly when jumping into the Arena from the starting perch. If you don't, Aloy takes a second or two to get up, which can hamper your advantage against the machines, who are instantly alerted to you as soon as you get close to the ground.

Like in Frozen Wilds, you can tell an Apex machine from a distance thanks to their purple HEPHAESTUS cables, as well as their new black armor plating.

Your difficulty setting and Aloy's level determines how often Apex machines appear. So the best way to encounter Apex machines more often is to level Aloy up and bump up the difficulty setting a notch or two.

Apex machines can never be overridden. While you can complete Cauldrons to unlock the ability to override many machines, you cannot do this with their black and purple Apex variants.

You can ambush a machine convoy by parking your Mount in their way on the road. The convoy will stop and won't attack your Mount, giving you the perfect opportunity to lie in wait and attack precisely the way you want to.

While Rebels often wear masks to protect themselves from being killed with a single headshot, we've discovered that if you use Concentration, it's possible to quickly shoot off their mask before landing a kill shot to the head. If you do this fast enough, the Rebel won't have enough time to raise the alarm!

Aloy's shots cannot penetrate water, so be mindful when firing at submerged machines.

THINGS TO DO FIRST IN HORIZON FORBIDDEN WEST

Mainline the Early Quests to Unlock Special Gear

Once you arrive in The Daunt via the cable car, you'll find there's a lot to do in this relatively small area. However, instead of exploring, we recommend mainlining several early Main Quests - Tap to Reveal - as they unlock handy tools that are needed to explore the many hidden nooks and crannies the game has to offer.

Complete This Early Errand to Get a Powerful Free Weapon

Though yes, mainlining the early quests mentioned above will do you well, there are a few things worthwhile in The Daunt, Horizon Forbidden West's first area. Looking to earn one of the best, free weapons that you'll discover during the early hours of the game? Well, to unlock this weapon, you'll need to complete the Errand Quest, A Bigger Boom, that's found when visiting Chainscrape, the first major settlement you visit in The Daunt.

When reaching the settlement, make your way towards the western gate, and you'll discover two Oseram tinkers that offer to build a powerful new weapon, should you help find the right parts. After helping gather the required machine parts, the two tinkers will construct a Spike Thrower, a unique weapon that launches Explosive Spikes that detonate after a short delay.

Not only is this weapon powerful, but it'll be a key part of your arsenal for quite some time, as you won't unlock rarer, more powerful weapons until further into the story.

Get This Other Free Stuff, Too

Stop by the Hunting Grounds in the Daunt and talk to the Grounds Keeper to get a free Shock Warrior Bow!

Complete bother parts of the Side Quest called The Bristlebacks to get a free rare Outfit.

Unlock the Smoke Bombs Recipe by Helping Some Vanguards in The Daunt

When reaching The Daunt, you can score yourself two free Smoke Bombs by helping a Vanguard couple that has been ambushed by some Scroungers while clearing up Bristleback carcasses. Upon helping defeat the machines and freeing the Vanguard soldier, you'll be rewarded for your time with the two Smoke Bombs, as well as the ability to craft them.

Finding this event isn't that easy, as it will not appear on the world map. To find and help this couple, locate the Charger Mount Site just south of Chainscrape. From the Chargers, continue a short distance south to the nearby Campfire. Then, follow the path east, past the Vista Point Tower, and across the small stream, where you'll soon hear the commotion of the fight.

Get Yourself a Mount As Soon As Possible

Make traveling easier and grab yourself a Mount, as you'll have the ability to Override Chargers as soon as you step foot in The Daunt.

See How to Override and Mount Machines

Do note, you'll want to avoid calling your Mount when in stealth, as once it nears your location, it will attract the attention of any nearby machines – and trust, it never ends well.

Visit Settlements and Pick Up Some Handy Weapons

As you begin to explore, you'll discover settlements of all different sizes. While you won't be able to view what's inside until you enter them, you'll find everything from activities such as Machine Strike and Melee Pits, Side Quests, and Merchants that range from Hunting Goods (Weapons), Stitchers (Outfits), Painters (Face Paints), and even Dyers,

It's worth checking in on new settlements that you discover, as each merchant will sell several unique items, such as Weapons, Outfits, and even rare Machine Parts.

Before traveling into the Forbidden West, stop by the Hunting Goods shop in Barren Light and purchase a Fire Hunter Bow; it'll come in handy for tackling some of the more powerful machines beyond The Daunt that are weak against the fire element. With that said, you'll want to make it a goal to have access to weapons of all elemental types eventually.

Sync with Tallnecks to Uncover Large Chunks of the Map

Whenever you get to a new area, beeline it to Tallnecks. Syncing up with a Tallneck will lift the fog of war and reveal a vast chunk of the map while also marking points of interest. This will help you get a lay of the land and cut down on time spent wandering around, hoping something will be revealed on the map.

Unlock Any Nearby Campfires and Shelters as you Explore

One thing you'll quickly learn is just how massive the Forbidden West truly is, and as you can imagine, navigating this world won't be quick. So, while you're exploring the open world, be sure to uncover any campfires and shelters that you may pass along the way, as it'll allow you to Fast Travel around the map, should you ever need to return to the area in the future.

Grab Yourself Some Fast Travel Packs

While Fast Travel may be free from Campfires, we highly recommend picking up some Fast Travel Packs from Merchants or crafting them yourself should you have the resources.

Costing just 25 Metal Shards from most Hunting merchants, these Fast Travel Packs will allow you to open the world map and travel just about anywhere. These come in handy when a Campfire may not be close by and even when unfortunate bugs or glitches prevent you from moving from a certain location.

Alternatively, holding Down on the D-Pad will bring up Aloy's Hunter Kit, where you'll then have the ability to craft Fast Travel Packs for 10 Ridge-Wood and 3 Wild Meat.

Explore Relic Ruins to Earn Easy XP and Valuable Rewards

Once operated by the Old Ones, Relic Ruins will see you completing Tomb Raider and Uncharted style environment puzzles. Unfortunately, most of these ruins will require you to use Special Gear Tools, which are unlocked fairly early within the Main Questline, but the Relic Ruin in The Daunt does not!

With no combat involved, these environment puzzles only require some critical problem-solving, as they'll see you navigating the environment to reach valuable loot caches and Collectible Ornaments.

So, if you're looking to take a quick breather from machine hunting, Relic Ruins will not only earn you some hefty XP but also plenty of valuable rewards.

Upgrade Your Pouches

Don't delay upgrading your pouches, as most of the early inventory upgrades require Key Upgrade Resources from wildlife that are often found roaming the earlier regions of the game.

Learn Potion Crafting Recipes

To unlock the ability to craft Potions, you'll first need to obtain the Potion you're trying to craft by purchasing it from a Merchant or finding one as you explore the open world.

Once you've obtained the particular Potion you're looking for, you'll unlock its crafting recipe, which will allow you to craft that specific potion via your Hunter's Kit, should you have the necessary space to store it in your Potion Pouch.

Consider Changing These Settings

When first jumping into Horizon Forbidden West, we highly recommend checking the Settings menu, as you'll find plenty of unique features and accessibility options that can affect the way you approach the game, especially during combat and exploration situations.

With features ranging from Climbing Annotations always being on, increasing the Weapon Wheel Slowdown and Concentration Duration, automatically sprinting, healing or using the Shieldwing, or even Co-Pilot, which enables the use of a second controller with mirrored controls, there's a high chance you'll find something that you'll want to tweak.

Discover Your Playstyle and Don't Horde Your Skill Points

As you progress through the game, you'll begin to earn Skill Points through things such as leveling up, completing Quests, and unlocking content within particular Activities. Earning these Skill Points can often go unnoticed; however, you can find out how many Skill Points you have available to spend by viewing the upwards-facing arrow that's found in the top right of your HUD.

The order or skill tree in which you choose to invest your skill points is entirely up to you, as each of the six skill categories – Warrior, Trapper, Hunter, Survivor, Infiltrator, and Machine Master – are designed to accommodate a particular playstyle.

While there is no right or wrong decision, just make sure you choose wisely, as skill points can not be refunded. However, do note you will eventually earn enough skill points to complete each of the categories. If you want some additional advice on what to unlock first, check out our page on Best Skills.

Complete Your First Cauldron and Unlock Machine Overrides and New Mounts

Much like the original game, Horizon Forbidden West features several Cauldrons that you can explore and override their cores to learn unique machine Overrides. Each Cauldron will unlock a number of unique machines that you can override, as well as mount.

Complete Activities to Unlock Unique Cosmetics, Weapons, and Outfits

These are, of course, optional, but might be on your personal list of things you want to do first. Wanting to spruce up Aloy's Outfit with a new color or rock a new Face Paint? Complete Main Quests, Side Quests, Errands, and Activities to unlock unique Dyes, Face Paints, and more. Tip: If you check your Quest log, you'll be able to view the rewards you'll receive for completing each quest you have discovered.

Do note that some quests – such as Tap to Reveal, which is unlocked in Camp Nowhere – will lead you through areas that sometimes have hidden Superior Loot Caches you'll need to pry open.

These loot caches will contain either a Weapon or Outfit, often of high rarity. Unfortunately, these loot caches are not included in the quest rewards and can be easily missed!

Complete Hunting Grounds and Earn Medals (These Will Be Extremely Useful Later in the Game)

It is highly recommended that you check out each Hunting Ground as you encounter them. They act as fast travel points, the Grounds Keepers sometimes give you free weapons or tools, and completing the trials grants rewards that can later be used to purchase Very Rare Weapons and Outfits via a store that is unlocked when completing the Side Quest, Tap to Reveal.

Furthermore, Hunting Grounds are a great way to refresh your combat skills if you're returning from Horizon Zero Dawn or jumping into the series for the first time, as you'll learn handy strategies and tips that you'll utilize throughout the game.

For even more on Horizon Forbidden West, don't forget to check out our Essential Tips and Tricks Guide, Things Horizon Forbidden West Doesn't Tell You, as well as our Beginner's Guide that covers all the basics you need to know about Forbidden West.

THINGS HORIZON FORBIDDEN WEST DOESN'T TELL YOU

In a world with so much to do and explore, it's easy for helpful features in Horizon Forbidden West to slip through the cracks and go unexplained. Whether it's small updates that expand on the first game – like fast travel at campfires or uncovering additional dialogue with NPCs after completing quests – to more useful tips and tricks – such as not topping off your ammunition or adjusting the time of day – this guide breaks down over 40 of the most noteworthy features that aren't explained well and that you may not have realized were possible in Horizon Forbidden West.

Check the Settings

Be sure to check the Settings menu, as you'll find plenty of unique features and accessibility options that can affect the way you approach the game, especially during combat and exploration situations. These features range from Climbing Annotations always being on, increasing the Weapon Wheel Slowdown and Concentration Duration, automatically sprinting, healing or using the Shieldwing, or even Co-Pilot, which enables the use of a second controller with mirrored controls.

Superior Chest Colors
Don't be deceived by the color of markers on golden Superior Chests! Any chest that you have to pry open will always contain some armor or a weapon, so it's always worth opening regardless of its rarity color.

How Fast Travel Works
The Fast Travel mechanics have changed since Zero Dawn. There's no Golden Fast Travel Pack anymore, but to make up for it you can now use Campfires and Shelters to Fast Travel for free. See How to Fast Travel and Change the Time of Day for more details, but for a summary:

You can Fast Travel to more than just Campfires! Hunting Grounds, Tallnecks, Relic Ruins, Salvage Contractors, Gauntlet Runs, Sunken Caverns, and more can be Fast Traveled to directly by selecting their icon on the map. Rebel Outposts and Camps can also be Fast Traveled to after you capture them.

You can also Fast Travel to a Settlement by selecting its zoomed out icon; there's no need to zoom in and then pick its Campfire.

Early into the story you'll unlock a location known as Tap to Reveal, a location you can Fast Travel to from anywhere without needing a Fast Travel Pack Since it drops you off near a Campfire, you can use this as a "nexus point" to bypass Fast Travel Packs altogether. Simply Fast Travel to The Base for free, then Fast Travel via the Campfire!

Easily Collect Datapoints

Scrounging for Datapoints? Use your Focus! Not only will they be highlighted with a large pink glow, you can even scan them for their data from a distance, and even through walls!

- When you highlight an Audio Datapoint with your Focus, you can press Triangle to listen to it while in gameplay, rather than in a menu. In some cases this will allow Aloy to comment on them once they've finished playing!

Explore Underwater

- Pools of water can lead to many hidden secrets to uncover. Beneath the surface of these pools, you may just discover valuable loot caches, as well as hidden cavern entrances that are marked by glowing blue mushrooms – this glow is hard to miss and can be spotted from above the surface. When exploring these Sunken Caverns and more, you'll find rare and valuable resources such as Greenshine Sliver and more.
- Eventually, you'll be able to stay underwater for longer with a tool unlocked by progressing through the Main Story Missions, so don't sweat about not being able to fully explore everything. See Blocked Paths - How to Unlock All Tools for more info.

How to Call a Mount

- Once you've Overridden a Mount, you don't have to unlock the ability to call it at any time like in Zero Dawn. Instead, select the Mount Whistle in your Hunter's Tools and call for it by pressing Down on the D-Pad. If you can't find the Mount Whistle, then you currently don't have a Mount (because it got destroyed, not because you got too far from it).
- Never look at where your Mount is before summoning it. If your Mount is off-screen, then it'll teleport to about 20 meters away before galloping towards you. However, if your Mount is on-screen, it will manually get over to you and will be at the mercy of its pathfinding AI, which can take a lot longer!

All About Mounts

Be careful when fighting near your Mount! While Aloy's melee range is already pretty wide, the button for Light Attack is also the button for Critical Strike. If your Mount is downed and needs to be revived, this can cause a Light Attack to instead Critical Strike the Mount, instantly killing it!

- Overridden Machines won't move when you shoot components off them. This is really handy for harvesting resources - especially once you unlock new override codes for bigger machines at cauldrons! Be careful, however, as every time you attack a friendly machine, it will decrease the override timer, meaning you'll have to defend yourself from it eventually!
- Mount faster by summoning your Mount whilst running, it will try to catch up to you so you can hop on mid-run. While this is very handy for quick getaways, it's also faster than calling

for it while standing still, where it will take a moment or two to reach you. Doing so while running also guarantees you'll start traveling in your intended direction!

The blue-and-white icon above your Mount indicates its loyalty. Every time it takes damage, the meter will decrease. When it runs out, your Mount will now be hostile towards you. If it hasn't turned on you, a Mount's loyalty can be restored by repairing it.

Need to stop your Mount quickly? Hold down the slow button and can go from a full sprint to a dead stop. Conversely, you can hold down the accelerate button to go faster and faster, rather than pressing it four times.

Mounts have Auto-Pilot, just like in Zero Dawn. While riding a Mount, if you let go of the Left Analog Stick while moving, they'll automatically follow the path, and even try to take the route to an activated Quest if you have one. Just be careful of corners at high speeds, as mounts are rather terrible at that. To make adjustments, or to take full control again, simply use the Left Stick again.

Enhance Valor Surges

Once you've purchased a Valor Surge, you can upgrade it with Skill Points so that it becomes more useful. For example, with the Level 3 Stealth Stalker, stealth kills restore Valor so that you can remain invisible for longer, letting you chain stealth kills together far more easily. See How to Unlock and Use Valor Surges for even more detailed info about Valor Surges.

Don't Top Off Ammunition!

Don't "Top off" your ammunition. Crafting a new batch of ammo will cost the same regardless of your ammo cap. For example, crafting a pack of Shock Light Arrows will cost (among other things) 3 Shock Canisters to make 7 arrows. If you have 12 / 14 shots and then craft a pack of arrows, it will still cost 3 Shock Canisters despite only making 2 arrows!

Unlock More Dialogue and Datapoints

Check up on people after finishing Quests; they often have new things to say after you've finished. For example, after completing "The Twilight Path", you can talk to Petra again (who gave you that quest in the first place) to hear her reactions to your success. You can even find new Datapoints this way!

Skipping certain Side Quests could have you miss out on dialogue options and cutscene beats later on in the main quest. For a non-spoilery early example, the finale of the Chainscrape storyline will directly mention any of the Side Quests you completed in that area as part of the scene!

What Are ? Icons

If you're looking for Old World activities (that aren't Relic Ruins), keep an eye out for "?" icons with a flat top. These indicate old-world sites while "?" with a rounded top indicates "modern" points of interest.

How to Learn New Crafting Recipes

- Despite having the resources available, you'll first need to learn the crafting recipes for Potions before you're able to craft them in your Hunter's Kit. To learn a Potion crafting recipe, you'll need to either purchase a Potion from a merchant or find one in the world. So, if you happen to come by any Potions that you don't have unlocked, we highly recommend you pick it up, even if it's purely for the purpose of learning the recipe. This is the same for other tools, like Smoke Bombs.
- How to Sneak Faster
- Aloy will slide down slopes a long way (to Slide, hit the Crouch button while Sprinting). You can use this to quickly slip by machines, since Aloy is low to the ground and is technically crouching. To cancel the Slide early, press the Crouch button again and Aloy will return to crouching low to the ground, handy for stopping right inside tall grass.
- Get Through Dialogue Faster
- Press X to skip through a few seconds during dialogue scenes. Just be careful though as X is also the button to choose a dialogue option, so avoid moving the left stick as you go!

Get a Closer Look with the Bow

- If you need to zoom in to get a better view of something, pull out your Bow with L2, then use R3 (click down on the Right Analog Stick); this will enter Concentration, which zooms the view in enough for you to get a better view, without nocking an arrow!
- Save Ammo By Canceling a Shot
- If you've drawn your bow and notched an arrow ready to fire, but change your mind, simply let go of L2: Aloy will lower her bow without firing the arrow. This is the same for other types of ranged weapons, too.
- Try Outpacing NPCs
- NPCs still keep up with your movement speed! One of the hallmark details from Zero Dawn is still in Forbidden West, where NPCs match your speed (usually): they'll walk, jog or sprint along with you so that you don't have to worry about leaving them behind or them escaping into the distance.
- Swimming and the Oxygen Meter
- When swimming, using L3 to "sprint" uses more oxygen, as well as using Circle to lunge. Conversely, it will barely deplete at all if you're still, giving you time to examine your surroundings.
- The breath meter is actually quite forgiving when you're trying to surface for air: it lasts about 10 seconds longer than the meter indicates, giving you some extra time to surface.

Change the Time of Day at Will

- Unlike in Zero Dawn, you can actually change the time of day in Forbidden West. Find a Shelter (marked with a fire icon with two lines above it on the map) and sit on a stump to choose to make it Morning, Afternoon, Evening or Night. This is very useful if you have trouble seeing the gameplay at nighttime.

Restock Your Pouch, Instantly

You can summon Medicinal Berries from your inventory to your Medicine Pouch! When you don't have a full medicine pouch, hold Up on the D-Pad and it'll be topped up using your inventories stash of 30 Medicinal Berries.

How Healing Medicine Works

When you use healing medicine, it will keep adding health until you're full, or you run out of medicine. This process can use up more than one medicine: each "tab" of the health bar equals one medicine.

Pause in Cutscenes With Photo Mode

You can use Photo Mode in cutscenes! While you are much more limited in what you can do (no pose or face options, for example), it is very helpful in getting just the right shot during the scene rather than hoping you timed your capture press right.

How to Choose Dialogue Options

When a dialogue option is white, that means there's new information to hear, and will turn gray when you've heard everything there is to learn. But this applies to options that you've already chosen too: if an option turns from gray back to white, that means choosing it will have the same scene play out, but revised to reflect new events and information. In rare cases, this can happen mid-conversation!

Check The Base Often for Free Rare Stuff

As you progress through the main story and reach The Base, you'll unlock a high-value supply cache that is continually filled with rare resources after you complete new quests. Given the ease of travel in Forbidden West, we highly recommend checking in on the supply cache regularly and removing any free resources it may have to provide. From our experience, our superior supply caches have been filled with rare Coils, Weaves, Advanced Traps, and other helpful resources.

Reading the ? Suspicious Icons

If a machine or human is suspicious of you (or in the "yellow state"), a yellow icon with a ? appears at the top of the screen. If you lose sight of the machine, the icon will gain a white ring: when this ring depletes the enemy will give up searching for you and return to normal.

How to Time Melee Combos

- If you're performing a melee combo that requires a pause in the middle, look for the glint that appears on the spear (you'll also hear a sheen sound from your TV and controller). Hit the next button input right on this glint to successfully continue the combo. You'll have to unlock melee combos first in the Skills menu!

Throwing a Rock Isn't Always the Answer

- If you throw a rock to distract it, the machine will keep looking in your direction until it reaches the rock's location. If the machine is too close, throwing the rock will instead give you away!

Tag Multiple Components at Once

- When scanning a machine with the Focus, you can Tag multiple Components on the same machine!

Reviving Allies Is Time Sensitive

- When reviving someone like a party member or Mount, the timer for when they die does NOT pause if you start Reviving them! If there's not enough time, you'll have to face facts and abandon them.

Shieldwing Top Tip

Because the Shieldwing has a delay before activating, press the Square button as early in the jump as you can: Aloy will deploy it at the top of her jump, ensuring you get the maximum glide distance.

Activate Hidden Side Quests

In larger settlements, like those with a Stitcher and Herbalist, Side Quests markers may not show up on the map until you're actually in or near the settlement itself.

Sell Valuables Confidently

While certain weapon upgrades need machine Hearts, only those needed to craft something (like Behemoth or Thunderjaw Hearts) are kept out of the "Valuables to Sell" section of your Inventory. Thus you can sell any Hearts that do appear there without worry.

Catch Fish Without Killing Them

You don't have to kill fish to catch them! If you're fast, you can Boost with the Square button to catch up with them: when you're close, press Triangle to catch them for their resources!

Consider Changing Valor Surges Carefully

Be careful when changing your Valor Surges. If you have a Level 3 Valor Surge but then switch to a Level 1 Valor Surge, your Valor will be reduced to fill only a Level 1 bar. That's bad for when you change your mind and switch to a Level 2 or 3 Valor Surge, since you just deleted a lot of hard-earned Valor!

Encounter Apex Machines More (or less)
Apex machines are extra-difficult forms of machines that drop the most valuable and rare loot and resources in the game. How often they appear is determined by your difficulty setting and Aloy's level, so the best way to encounter Apex enemies more often is to level Aloy up and bump up the difficulty a notch or two.

Free Rare Machine Parts
Throughout the Forbidden West, you'll discover fallen machines that are surrounded by Rebels scrounging for machine parts. Should you kill these Rebels, they'll drop the parts they have managed to scavenge from the machine, such as the Legendary parts. This is an easy way to obtain rare parts without actually killing the machine in question.

Cars Are Basically Loot Boxes
Certain Old One's vehicles such as cars and buses have panels that you can either hit or Pry Open, revealing boxes of loot. Use your Focus to highlight these panels in yellow

Assist in Unmarked Events for Rewards
Look out for unmarked events that occur throughout the world. These events could involve helping NPCs defeat a machine or even clearing Rebels from Campfires. Remember to stick around and talk to the NPC leading these events, as your rewards can range from free traps, resources, and even dyes!

BEST SKILLS

Horizon Forbidden West's skill trees are a testament to the wide variety of play styles you can choose to tackle the many challenges ahead. This skills guide will help you decide which skills to choose first in Horizon Forbidden West, and will suggest some of the best skills available.

Keep in mind, as suggested above, your playstyle will largely affect which skills appeal to you. If you never rely on traps, skills in the Trapper tree will likely not work well for you, for example.

How to Get Skill Points
Earn Skill Points by completing all variations of Side Quests, Main Quests, and pretty much all other activities from clearing Rebel Camps to climbing Tallnecks, or just by leveling up.

Can I Reset Skill Points?

You won't be able to refund Skill Points once you spend them, but do know you will eventually be able to fully unlock every skill tree if you make an effort doing side activities.

SPOILER WARNING: You can see the entirety of every Skill Treee in Horizon Forbidden West as soon as you finish the tutorial, but here's a warning just in case!

Skill Trees Explained

Warrior Skill Tree	Trapper Skill Tree	Hunter Skill Tree
Warrior skills primarily focus on new melee combos and passive damage boosts for your spear, but also include new Weapon Techniques for the close-range Warrior Bows. The Active Skills really do make a big difference with how the spear handles.	Trapper skills make setting and crafting traps faster and easier, plus provide some defense against your own traps. Find Weapon Techniques for the Ropecaster and Tripcaster. Also find passive boosts for food effects here.	Hunter skills boost a pretty large variety of things, including concentration, valor surge buildup, and weapon stamina (which allows you to use Weapon Techniques). Save resources when crafting ammo for all weapons, and do more damage with the heavy weapons knocked from machines. There are Weapon Techniques for the Hunter Bow and Boltblaster, too.

Survivor Skill Tree	Infiltrator Skill Tree	Machine Master Skill Tree
Survivor skills make surviving, well, easier, with passive health regen, defense, and medicine boosts. Also deal more damage when you're critically injured, and learn Active Skills for the Shredder Gauntlets and Blastling.	Embrace stealth with Infiltrator skills. Do more damage while in stealth, and become more difficult for enemies to notice you. Increase Smoke Bomb capacity for gaffs, buff Silent Strike in various ways, and learn Weapon Techniques for the Sharpshot Bow.	Machine Master skills make your overridden machine buddies better with passive boosts and an additional behavior option. The Valor Surges here make it loads easier to fight machines, too, as do the Spike Thrower Weapon Techniques.

Best Skills to Get First

Before we get into our suggested best essential skills, consider how you like to play Horizon. Stealthy archer? Close-up melee? Trapper? Luckily, the skill trees are neatly arranged loosely based on playstyle, but there are some skills here and there that will benefit everyone regardless. Just keep your own preferences in mind when reading this list!

Resonator Blast (Warrior) - Often you won't have a choice when up against other people, you'll have to get up close and personal. The Resonator Blast is an extremely important skill to have when facing people. It "energizes" your spear, and then leaves your opponent with a weak spot you can shoot with a bow. You'll also have to learn this to participate in the Pit Challenges. The first is in Chainscrape, where you'll have to successfully perform a Resonator Blast.

Melee Damage (Warrior) - This is a no-brainer. Whether you prefer relying on your spear or not, everyone uses it sometimes - and a passive damage buff is undeniably great. Suggesting this is also a bit of a cheat on our part, because you "have" to unlock Block Breaker, a useful melee combo, in order to get to it. Want more passive Melee boosts? Continue the Warrior Skill Tree all the way on the right, and unlock Power Attack + and Burst Fire to reach another Melee Damage passive boost - which will buff your melee damage a whopping 70%! However, this is a bit of an investment, and melee isn't the best to use against machines since they can't be relied on to tear off important resources, so maybe wait to upgrade this one for a while.

Part Breaker (Machine Master Valor Surge) - Part Breaker is a Valor Surge, which is a temporary buff you can trigger after building enough "valor" meter. See How to Unlock and Use Valor Surges for more info on those in general.

This Valor Surge, Part Breaker, makes it much easier to remove machine components, which are necessary to upgrade and purchase weapons and outfits. That's not all, as when upgraded to Tier 3, Part Breaker makes it so the machine will be knocked down every time you tear off a component with it active. This skill pairs very well with Stealth Tear + - sneak up on your opponent, highlight the part you need with your Focus, activate Part Breaker, and knock components off in a flash. Then, while it's knocked down, finish the kill with a critical strike! For tough bosses, this helps eliminate their heavy weapons fast, too!

Stealth Tear + (Infiltrator) - For the same reasons above, any skills that help you gather machine components are winners in our book. Focus down the component you need while in stealth before inciting the chaos of battle.

Stealth Ranged + (Infiltrator) If you like doing headshots (on humans, usually in Rebel Camps), this is the skill for you. Both of these Stealth skills are very cheap to unlock, too, as they're at the very beginning of the Infiltrator tree.

Potent Medicine (Survivor) - If you find yourself eating Medicinal Berries to recover in a pinch often, the very first skill in the Survivor line will serve you well. This passive boost makes Medicinal Berries provide 20% more healing and healing speed, saving "you" and resources simultaneously.

- **Valor Surge Master (Hunter)** - This is a passive boost that lets you build valor faster, allowing you to perform more powerful Valor Surges more often! The two Concentration skills you need to unlock to get here, surprise surprise, also pairs well with Part Breaker.
- **Quick Wire (Trapper)** - Another mildly cheeky suggestion, but if you like traps, you definitely need this one.

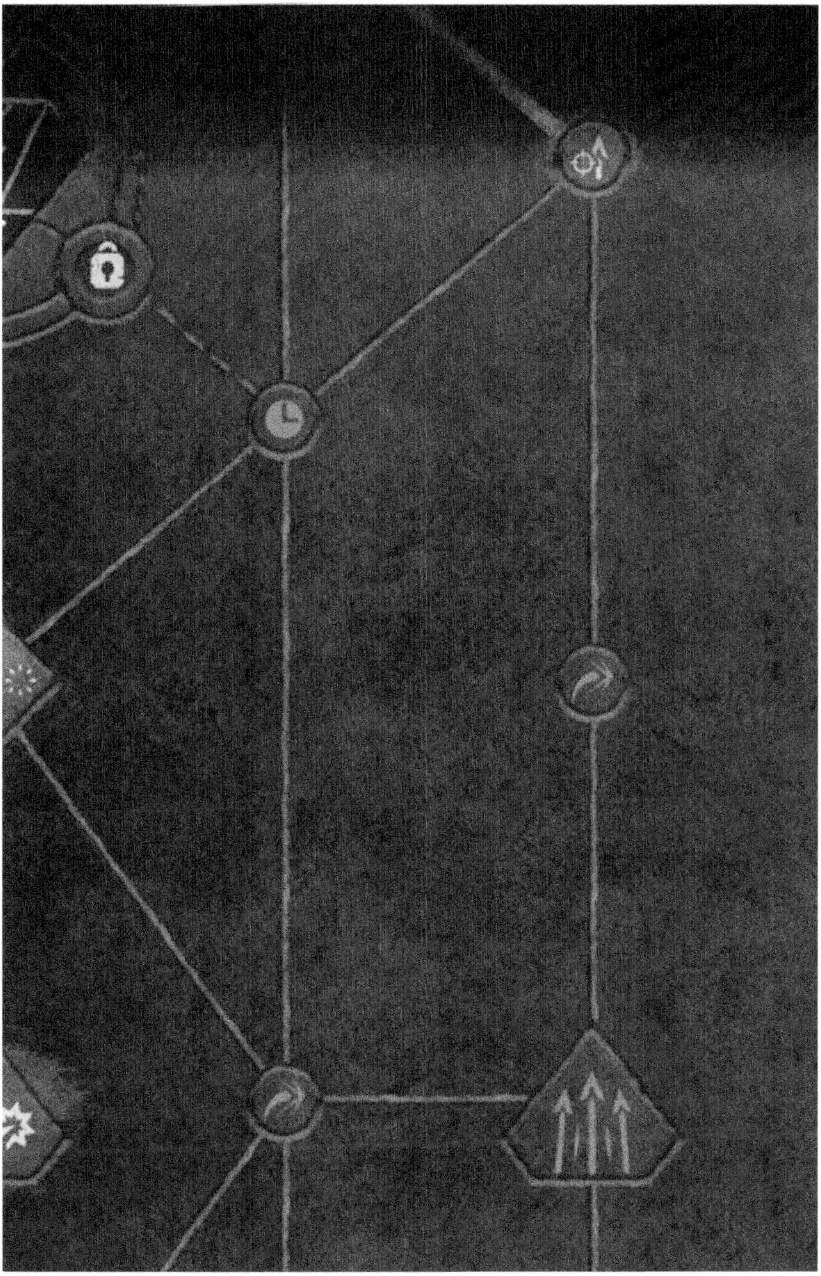

Quick Wire launches a Tripcaster's Tripwire instantly, removing the need to manually put down both points yourself. Find this skill on the left side of the Trapper tree. On the way, you'll have to unlock Quick Trapper, Skilled Salvager, and Trap Limit (which lets you place 3 traps or tripwires at a time instead of just 2), all essential skills for even the most basic trapper.

Those are plenty to get you started, but since the entirety of all Skill Trees are visible immediately, check them out and make a loose plan! Or, hold onto your Skill Points for a bit until you feel like you need a buff in a particular area. It will take a while to really figure out your favorite way to play, after all. Just keep in mind the Pit Challenges and the related Errand called The Enduring will require you to unlock certain Warrior skills to participate, but some Hunting Ground Trials will certainly benefit from skills on other trees, too.

Passive Skill Buffs

The following are all passive skills, meaning they are always active and provide buffs.

Resource, Valor, and Health Boosts

Ammo Expert (Hunter) - This allows you to craft more ammunition from the same amount of resources, which is incredibly helpful for saving on supplies and will greatly reduce your need to restock as frequently.

Medicine Capacity (Survivor) - Increases the amount of Medicine that you can carry on you.

Potent Medicine / Potion Proficiency (Survivor) - Improves the amount and speed of healing medicine/potions.

Plant Forager (Survivor) - Lets you gather more resources from plants, especially helpful for healing medicine or saving up for dyes.

Valor on Impact (Survivor) Gives you Valor when you're hit by an enemy, which will help make the most out of any mistakes you make.

Plant Forager (Survivor) - Lets you gather more resources from plants, especially helpful for healing medicine or saving up for dyes.

Stealth and Concentration Boosts

- **Concentration +, Deep Concentration and Concentration Regen (Hunter)** - Lengthens the duration you can slow down time with Concentration. It is a must for any archer as it makes it easier to hit machine components or land headshots.
- **Silent Strike + (Infiltrator)** - Increases the damage dealt by a Silent Strike, making it more likely that it will kill the target (as indicated by the skull icon in the Silent Strike button prompt)
- **Stealth Tear + (Hunter)** Increases your Tear Damage by a certain percentage. In tandem with Concentration, you can more easily kill a machine by sniping the right components this way.

Stealth Ranged + (Infiltrator) - Passively deal more Impact Damage when using a bow in stealth, which is very helpful when trying to headshot human opponents in a stealth run.
Low Profile and Quiet Movement (Infiltrator) - Passively reduces Aloy's visibility/noise. This is useful for any build as it lets you more easily skulk around the battlefield to scope things out, covertly lay traps, tail enemies, and position yourself to attack at the right time and place.

Combat Boosts

Critical Strike + (Warrior) - When you've knocked an enemy (or a boss) down, dealing more damage with a Critical Strike can be very useful.
Melee Damage - You fight human enemies with melee a lot, so passive buffs are always helpful in taking them down quickly.

Handy Active Skills

Resonator Blast (Warrior Skill Tree) - The first skill in the Warrior Skill tree is a must-unlock, even for those that prefer to use their bow. With the right combo, the Resonator Blast allows you to build up energy on your spear, and when fully charged, it can be used to energize your opponent. When shooting the energy marked on your opponent with your bow, you'll deal a large amount of damage, which can be increased via a passive boost further down the Skill Tree.
The Destroyer (Warrior) - While it's expensive to drill down to, this is a *very* fast melee combo and is great at quickly tearing down enemy health.

Must-Have Weapon Techniques

Quick Wire (Trapper) - If you're a Tripcaster user, this ability instantly fires a complete length, great for in the heat of battle.
Triple Notch (Hunter) - If you focus more on impact damage, this is great for quickly dealing more damage with Hunter Bows. Is also great on resilient machine components like on Apex machines. Alternatively, the **Double Notch (Infiltrator)** is a great option for those that specialize in long-range Sharpshot Bows.
Focused Shot (Infiltrator) - Increases the zoom on your next Sharpshot Bow shot and increases the damage, which is very useful in shooting resilient components and/or hitting targets across long distances.
Knockdown Shot (Hunter) - Lets your next Hunter Bow shot knock down enemies, meaning it pairs really well with Critical Strike +.
Sticky Bomb (Survivor) - Lets you stick multiple Blastsling bombs to a target. Notably, sticking several bombs to an enemy at once will deal more total damage than if you were to fire them all normally, making it great on enemies with a lot of health.

- **Override Subroutines (Machine Master)** - Lets you set a machine to Aggressive Behaviour. Use this on a machine at the start of a battle and they'll attack everyone else, making for a great distraction.

Suggested Valor Surges

- **Part Breaker Level 3 (Machine Master)** - Already highly recommended above, but as a reminder, Part Breaker makes it significantly easier to break off machine parts, which are needed to upgrade outfits and weapons. It also makes the damage you deal greater overall.
- **Overshield (Survivor)** - Replicates the original Shield-Weaver effect by making a shield that absorbs damage instead of Aloy, eliminating knockback. Upgraded versions deal a bit of damage to the attacker, while the Level 3 version will have the shield explode when it's depleted, great for enemies using melee attacks.
- **Stealth Stalker Level 3 (Infiltrator)** - Stealth Stalker turns Aloy invisible for a set period of time. The Level 3 version restores Valor for each stealth kill, allowing for stealth kill chains to be more easily achieved so long as your kills don't alert nearby enemies.
- **Powershots (Hunter)** - Lets your next few shots deal more damage and, with the upgraded versions, restores Concentration, making it great for fast sniping shots. Works with Bows, Boltblasters, Ropecasters and Spike Throwers.
- **Trap Specialist (Trapper)** - While rather situational at first, the Level 3 version of this Valor Surge launches hovering mines around Aloy which will blow up enemies when they get too close, making it great when taking on opponents who focus on melee attacks.
- **Chain Burst (Machine Master)** - Dealing damage to an enemy will also deal some damage to nearby enemies. If you're overpowered, this is especially great when attacking herd machines like deer, or when fighting human enemies close together. The Level 3 version will have the damage chain a second time!
- **Radial Burst (Infiltrator)** - Releases a powerful shockwave that damages all enemies in the vicinity, making it great as a crowd control move when you're being overwhelmed.

HOW TO UNLOCK AND USE VALOR SURGES

How to Unlock Valor Surges
Valor Surges must be unlocked in the Skills menu of Horizon Forbidden West. There are 12 different Valor Surges, two per skill tree.

In order to unlock a Valor Surge, you must first spend Skill Points on the skills surrounding it on the skill tree, like for this (highly recommended) Part Breaker Valor Surge in the image above. If a skill has a line connected to the Valor Surge point in the center, it must be unlocked. This makes unlocking these abilities quite expensive, but they're definitely powerful enough to be worth adding a few to your arsenal.

Spend additional skill points to level up Valor Surges, making them even more powerful. Do so by holding X to upgrade the skill while selecting it in the Skills menu.

How to Equip or Change Valor Surges
You can only equip one Valor Surge at a time. To do so, enter the Skills menu, navigate to a Valor Surge you have unlocked, and hold Square to equip it. Keep in mind if you have a Level 3 Valor Surge equipped and switch to a Level 1 or 2, you will not retain any of the valor you built up.

How to Use Valor Surges
Once you have a Valor Surge equipped, you should see a purple icon and bar on the bottom right of your screen. You can activate the Valor Surge by holding L1 and pressing R1, as long as you've built up enough valor in order to trigger it. (See this notification in the top right while holding L1).

You'll start out with one section of Valor Surge Bar, and more will be added with each level of upgrade your equipped Valor Surge is - up to three. A Valor Surge can be activated as soon as the first segment is filled, but this bar acts as a timer, so the longer you wait to activate it, the longer the Valor Surge will last.

How to Build the Valor Surge Bar
Valor must be earned by performing skilled, purposeful attacks and techniques, like the following. Keep in mind, these all stack! When you do something worthy of valor, it will notify you in purple text on the right side of the screen.

Action	Valor Points
Kill	15
Silent Strike	9
Component Removed	9
Elemental Limit Triggered	9
Weak Spot Hit	7
Knockdown	7
Stealth Kill	6
Shocked/Burning/etc. Kill (Killed while affected by an element)	6

Recommended Valor Surges

Here are some recommended Valor Surges with information on what they do and why they're useful. See the Best Skills page for more information on other recommended skills.

- **Part Breaker Level 3 (Machine Master)** - Increases the damage done to machine components and weak spots, meaning it pairs very well with Stealth Tear +. Given how quintessential machine components are to your progression in the game, the Part Breaker valor surge is especially useful to efficiently and literally rip through your machine enemies to both take them down and get the loot you need to buy and upgrade weapons and outfits. That's not all, as when upgraded to Level 3, any time you shoot off a component, the machine will be knocked down for a short period of time.
- **Overshield (Survivor)** - Replicates the original Shield-Weaver effect by making a shield that absorbs damage instead of Aloy, eliminating knockback. Upgraded versions deal a bit of damage to the attacker, while the Level 3 version will have the shield explode when it's depleted, great for enemies using melee attacks.
- **Stealth Stalker Level 3 (Infiltrator)** - Stealth Stalker turns Aloy invisible for a set period of time. The Level 3 version restores Valor for each stealth kill, allowing for stealth kill chains to be more easily achieved so long as your kills don't alert nearby enemies.
- **Powershots (Hunter)** - Lets your next few shots deal more damage and, with the upgraded versions, restores Concentration, making it great for fast sniping shots. Works with Bows, Boltblasters, Ropecasters and Spike Throwers.
- **Trap Specialist (Trapper)** - While rather situational at first, the Level 3 version of this Valor Surge launches hovering mines around Aloy which will blow up enemies when they get too close, making it great when taking on opponents who focus on melee attacks.
- **Chain Burst (Machine Master)** - Dealing damage to an enemy will also deal some damage to nearby enemies. If you're overpowered, this is especially great when attacking herd machines like deer, or when fighting human enemies close together. The Level 3 version will have the damage chain a second time!
- **Radial Burst (Infiltrator)** - Releases a powerful shockwave that damages all enemies in the vicinity, making it great as a crowd control move when you're being overwhelmed.

HOW-TO GUIDES

How to Fast Travel and Change the Time of Day

How to Fast Travel

To fast travel in Horizon Forbidden West, make your way to one of the many available Campfires, Shelters, or Settlements that can be found around the map. When visiting one of these sites, interact with the Campfire, and you will have access to fast travel to almost anywhere on the map. Do note you'll need to have traveled close enough to have unlocked Campfires and Activity locations to travel to them. Any icons faded grey will indicate they have not yet been unlocked.

If you're looking for something a little quicker, you have the option to craft or purchase Fast Travel Packs. To craft a Fast Travel Pack, hold Down on the D-Pad to bring up Aloy's Hunter Kit, where you'll then have the ability to craft Fast Travel Packs for 10 Ridge-Wood and 3 Wild Meat.

Alternatively, Fast Travel Packs cost just 25 Metal Shards and can be purchased from almost any Hunting merchant found throughout the Forbidden West. While Fast Travel Packs do cost supplies to craft and purchase, are they convenient for when a Campfire may not be close by and even when unfortunate bugs or glitches prevent you from moving from a certain location.

How to Change the Time of Day

Thankfully, changing the time of day in Horizon Forbidden West is fairly straightforward, as all you need to do is head to a Shelter and sit by the log that's next to the Campfire. Here, you'll have the option to progress time to any of the following options:

Morning

Afternoon

Evening

Night

After selecting one of the options, you'll watch in real-time as the time of day changes.

Tips and Tricks for Fast Traveling in Horizon Forbidden West

Lastly, here are some handy tips and tricks you may not know about Campfires, Shelters, and Fast Travel!

The following tips will contain minor spoilers for Main Quest and Settlement names beneath spoiler tags, so be warned.

The Fast Travel mechanics have changed since Zero Dawn. There's no Golden Fast Travel Pack anymore, but to make up for it, you can now use Campfires and Shelters to Fast Travel for free.

When stopping by Settlements and Shelters, keep an eye out for rare and valuable caches that are often scattered throughout the camps.

Early into the story, you'll unlock a location known as Tap to Reveal, a location you can Fast Travel to from anywhere without needing a Fast Travel Pack. Since it drops you off near a Campfire, you can use this as a "nexus point" to bypass Fast Travel Packs altogether. Simply Fast Travel to Tap to Reveal for free, then Fast Travel via the Campfire!

If you're about to drown and would rather not lose all the items you picked up while underwater, Fast Travel! You're still able to use Fast Travel Packs while swimming, letting you zip away to safety. If you do this to Tap to Reveal, it'll be for free!

How to Destroy Red Anomalous Crystal Growths (Firegleam)

Red Anomalous Crystal Growths, also known as Firegleam, can be found across the Horizon Forbidden West map. During the opening hours of the game, you'll likely come across this mysterious red crystal when exploring The Daunt and No Man's Land and probably wonder just how you can destroy them, as they're marked as a blocked path. In this guide below, we'll explain how to unlock the Special Gear item to destroy Red Anomalous Crystal Growths, as well as the requirements you'll need.

How to Destroy Red Anomalous Crystal Growths (Firegleam)

In short and without spoiling anything, you'll unlock the ability to destroy Red Anomalous Crystal Growths (Firegleam) by completing the first Main Quest that takes part in the Forbidden West, which sees Aloy crafting her second Special Gear item, the Igniter, a unique spear upgrade that allows the detonation of Firegleam. In addition, this tool can also be used to destroy obstacles, opening new paths in the environment.

It's also worth mentioning; this tool is not missable and is required to complete the Main Quest.

You're probably also curious as to what is hidden behind Firegleam? Well, it's nothing too exciting, as Firegleam is normally just blocking access to valuable resource caches and Greenshine – a rare resource that is used for upgrading weapons and outfits or purchasing rare coils, weaves, and machine parts from merchants.

If you're wanting to know exactly which Main Quest unlocks the Igniter, check the spoiler tag below.

Blocked Paths - How to Unlock All Tools

As you begin to explore the early hours of Horizon Forbidden West, you'll soon discover several icons and features within the world that you simply cannot access – including Metal Flowers and vines, Red Anomalous Crystal Growths, and even deep underwater caverns and structures. Sometimes, these are marked as "Blocked Path (Missing Tool Needed)." Here's how to get past blocked paths and unlock all four Special Gear tools that will allow you to explore the Forbidden West with no boundaries.

How to Unlock All Blocked Paths

Now that you have had a chance to explore the Forbidden West, you've probably uncovered several Blocked Paths that you cannot explore. Well, don't worry, as it's by design, as the game will see you crafting Special Gear tools throughout Main Quests.

Every tool that you need to unlock Blocked Paths will be unlocked through the main storyline of Horizon Forbidden West.

Now, sharing the names of these Main Quests could be considered spoilers, so we have listed further details below. You cannot miss these tools, and as along as you complete the story, you'll have them all unlocked by approximately the mid-point of Horizon Forbidden West

Just as another warning, clicking the spoiler tags below will reveal the name of the Main Quest, and at which point of the game, you will encounter the Quest that unlocks each particular tool. Apart from those minor spoilers, nothing more will be discussed.

SPOILER WARNING: Below, items that perform certain functions are discussed, as are main quest names.

Pullcaster

This is the first Special Gear you'll unlock. Aloy makes it during the tutorial Reach for the Stars and it's used to pull things, as its name suggests.

How to Override and Mount Machines
The ability to override machines has returned in Horizon Forbidden West, with Aloy now able to override up to 38 different types of machines. Throughout this guide, we'll break down everything you need to know about overriding machines, as well as unlocking additional mounts that Aloy can use for traversal or even combat.

How to Unlock Machine Overrides and More Mounts
To override machines, you must first locate any of the Tap to Reveal available Cauldrons found across the map. Keep in mind that each Cauldron is responsible for creating a set of unique machines typically found around the region.

Once you've located a Cauldron, you must fight your way through the facility as you attempt to reach and override its core. If you're successful, you'll learn overrides for several unique machines, along with potential mounts.

However, overriding works a little differently in Forbidden West, as not every machine you initially gain access to will be available to override straight away. Instead, when viewing the machine catalog via the Notebook, you'll find that a machine may be fully unlocked and ready to override, or just partially.

Should the machine be partially unlocked, you will be required to craft an override via the Fabrication Terminal found within Tap to Reveal. Once you've gathered the resources necessary and have crafted the override, you'll gain the ability to override the machine in the wild.

How to Override a Machine

Once a machine's override is unlocked, approach it stealthily and hold down Triangle when prompted. Depending on its override abilities, the machine will fight for you for a limited duration, or it will become available as a ridable mount.

Furthermore, should you unlock the Override Subroutines skill via the Machine Master Skill Tree, you'll have the ability to set a machine's behavior to be either aggressive or defensive when overriding.

How to Get Dyes and Dye Your Outfits

Looking to spruce up Aloy's Outfits with fancy new colorways? This guide breaks down not only breaks down how to find every outfit dye but also how to locate dye plants and even apply them to your outfits. Don't forget, you can change face paints, too!

How to Get Dyes

Unfortunately, there is no set way to obtain dyes in Horizon Forbidden West, as they are one of the few in-game items that are randomly unlocked or rewarded for the completion of Side Quests and Errands, Hunting Grounds, Salvage Contracts, Melee Pits, and unmarked events that you'll sometimes find across the map.

How to Find a Dyer and Apply Dyes to Outfits

Now that you have unlocked some dyes, you're probably wondering how to apply them to your Outfits. Throughout the Forbidden West, you will encounter merchants inside of Settlements, known as Dyers. Upon speaking with the Dyer, you will enter an interface showcasing your entire collection of Outfits, as well as their compatible dyes.

Be warned, as although you may have the dye unlocked, it will still require unique resources called Dye Plants to apply it.

To find Dye Plants, begin searching on rocky ledges and cliff faces; however, each particular region – whether it be the rainforest, mountains, desert, etc. - will each have its own unique plant. So we highly recommend creating jobs for any dye resources you are missing, as you'll receive a quest marker that will take you to the area of each dye's location.

How to Create Jobs and Get Upgrade Parts Quickly

Obtaining machine parts and resources has never been easier, as Horizon Forbidden West has implemented a brand-new job system that allows you to create mini-quest-like missions that will see you heading to the nearest location in which the parts and resources can be found.

To create a job, head to your nearest Workbench – these are typically found in Settlements and Shelters – and select the item you want to upgrade or craft, yet lack the necessary supplies needed. With the item selected, press Triangle, and you'll be prompted on whether you not you would like to set this job as your Active Quest.

When viewing the job, either via the in-game HUD or Quest Menu, you'll find an Objective List that details everything you need to obtain to make your requested upgrade.

Should you activate the quest, you'll receive markers on the world map that guide you to where resources can be found. While it won't pinpoint an exact location, it will provide an area radius where the machine, animal, or plants can be found.

Once you have obtained the necessary resources and materials, return to a workbench and craft your item!

How to Get and Use Face Paints
Face Paints are primarily earned by completing some Main Quests , Side Quests, and Errands,

but are also occasionally awarded for completing other activities. You'll get your first Face Paint pretty early on, from either the Deep Trouble side quest or The Embassy main quest. Despite unlocking a face paint early, you won't be able to use it for quite a while.

How to Use Face Paints

Unfortunately, Aloy isn't a makeup guru, and so she can't apply the face paints herself - however, if you just want to see what the Face Paint looks like, you can always equip it whenever you want in Photo Mode! It just won't persist once you leave the photography session.

Instead, for a more permanent makeover, she needs to visit a Painter. These are marked on the map with a primitive tattoo tool icon with "Painter (Face Paints)."

The first Painter won't be found until you head west to the town of Tap to Reveal, which you naturally won't run into until after completing the main quest interlude Tap to Reveal

Once you've completed that quest (where you'll find "The Base"), head directly west from there to find the first settlement with a painter.

Applying these Face Paints costs just 10 Metal Shards, but you'll have to pay each time you change Aloy's look.

You'll find a few more Painters further west, so keep an eye out. We'll update this page soon with exact locations.

SIDE QUESTS

This Horizon Forbidden West Side Quest guide is your handy tool for locating and completing all the side quests in the game. This guide will walk you through each side quest and will give you information about the recommended level, location of the side quests, and the rewards.

There are two ways to get a Side Quest: going into a settlement and following the bright green exclamation point on the map or listening to a rumor (marked on the map with a bright green exclamation point inside a bright green circle). Some Side Quests will not appear until you have completed a Main Quest or another Side Quest. For instance, The Bristleback's side quest is split into two parts; the second part will be accessible only after the Main Quest To the Brink has been completed.

Horizon Forbidden West includes Tap to Reveal that complement the Main Story Quests. Side quests are not as long as the Main Quests, but they are longer than Errands. Depending on the objectives, you can expect to spend about 45 minutes to an hour on a side quest. Most Side Quests will have you help someone in need and more often than not, you will have to fight some tough machines.

Side Quests are a great way to earn skill points and experience. In addition, you are often rewarded with rare weapons and outfits, and unique face paints. There are recommended levels for each Side Quest, as denoted in the chart below.

Deep Trouble
Getting Started

Deep Trouble is the first Side Quest you receive in Horizon Forbidden West. It is located in the Daunt in the mountains to the northwest of the lift landing. This quest will introduce you to The Daunt and the people who call this place home.

Upon arriving in The Daunt, Aloy travels to the northwest of the lift landing and finds a quarry, Crimson Narrows. There she encounters injured mineworkers and can see a smoking mine entrance. Speaking with the injured miners, Aloy learns that the mine has collapsed and the miners just managed to escape.

Their leader, Korvud, tells her that there are still two men trapped in the mine. Aloy offers to save them.

Find the Missing Miners

Enter the mine and go left. You will need to dive into the water and swim under the debris. There will be yellow handholds that you can use to propel you forward. Once you've cleared the debris, you will find yourself in a large cave. To the left, you will see a cache high up on a ledge, and in front of you will be a tunnel entrance under the water. To the right, there will be another tunnel entrance under the water.

You can try to get the cache on the high ledge, but it'll be easier to get later in the quest. The same goes for all the caches located under the water.

Dive into the water and choose either tunnel entrance. Whatever choice you make will still get you to the trapped miners. Clear the underwater tunnel and you will meet Thorden and his companion.

Get to the Cart and Drain the Mine

Thorden tells you that the cave-in was due to the miners' explosives and now that the whole area is flooded with water, they are unable to escape. Unfortunately, the only way to clear a path is to find a minecart, ignite the explosives in that cart, and push the cart into the rubble.

Thorden hands you the fuses you will need to clear the cave-in.

From Thorden's position, go left and dive into the water. You will need to swim through the underwater tunnel to get to the clearing where the minecart and the cave-in are. Once you are there, you will see the minecart on the track.

There are caches to get in this area, so explore for a bit to find them. Look for a short ladder directly under the minecart and climb up. Go left and jump the four beams.

Crouch through the tunnel and it will open up into a huge cavern. Below you will be three Burrowers. You can either choose to fight them or swim underneath to avoid them. Either way, you have to get to the far end of the cavern. You can also use the purple mushroom to provide a smoke cover if you want to be sneaky.

If you choose to fight the Burrowers, this fight will be fairly easy. Burrowers are weak against fire and basic arrow and melee shots. They have a stun ability so keep your distance if you can.

Once you've made your way to the far end of the cavern, go left, up, and around to find some minecart tracks. Follow the tracks until you get to a wall. Turn right and jump up the ledge. Go left and drop down. In front of you will be a ladder you can push down. This will be handy if you fall.

In front of the ladder is a wooden crane. Use your Pullcaster to pull the crane towards you (aim for the bright blue metal clamp). Jump and grab onto the yellow handles. Climb up and move forward. Jump the gap and grab onto the track and go right towards the minecart. There will be a few caches along the way so be sure to pick those up.

Once you are at the cart, place the fuses into the cart, and push the cart over the edge. The cart will explode, causing the rocks to tumble and the water to drain.

Leave the Mine
Now that you have cleared the water, drop down and make your way out of the cavern. Before you can leave, three Scroungers will appear. You will need to fight them to get out of the area. Fortunately, like the Burrowers, the Scroungers can be defeated easily. They are weak against frost and acid, but they are not strong against any type of attack. Arrows and melee attacks will make quick work of them. They are quick machines and have a shock attack that can stun you as well as a bite attack if they get too close.

After defeating them, make your way to the wall on the left and use your Pullcaster to pull the two crates away. Go through the opening and make your way back to Thorden.

With the water gone, Thorden and his companion can leave the mine. As you leave, you can open all the caches that you might have left behind. You can also use your Pullcaster to grab the big cache on the ledge that's on your way out.

The Bristlebacks Part 1
Getting Started
The Bristlebacks is a two-part quest that you receive in The Daunt. It is one of the few quests you start in one Main Quest line and finish in another. In this case, The Bristlebacks starts during the To the Brink Main Quest, but it can only be finished when you have completed The Embassy and the Tap to Reveal Main Quest begins.

When Aloy arrives in The Daunt, she meets a Carja Sun-Priest who is on his way to Barren Light, the location where the Embassy will occur. Aloy needs the Embassy to happen so that she can enter the Forbidden West. Unfortunately, the Sun-Priest refuses to move on as there are Bristlebacks everywhere. He has sent an old friend of Aloy's, Tap to Reveal, to fight off the Bristlebacks and clear a path.

Talk to Ulvund and Javad in Chainscrape

Unwilling to wait for Tap to Reveal and his group to clear a path, Aloy sets out for Chainscrape, the first main settlement in the Daunt. There she speaks to Ulvund, the unofficial official leader of Chainscrape. He tells her about the Bristleback problem and in response to it, he has shut down all work in the quarries outside of Chainscrape. Aloy goes to speak to the Carja magistrate, Javad the Willing, in an effort to get things moving along. Of course, he is unable to help her unless she uncovers the cause behind the recent surge of Bristleback activity.

Enter the Mine

Leave Chainscrape and head southwest. There will be a quarry, Split Crag, located in the mountains that shows signs of a Bristleback stampede. Enter the mine and move forward until you come to a cavern clearing. There will be Bristlebacks in the area that you will need to clear out. The Bristlebacks will be a bit of a challenge to defeat. They are big, bulky machines that can do a lot of damage if you are too close to them. Keep at a ranged distance from them or keep the high ground.

Return to Javad

Once they are eliminated, head to the far right of the cavern. You will see some smoke coming out of a tunnel. Go through the tunnel and turn left immediately. You will see a small table with a piece of paper on it. Use your Focus to scan the note to Ulvund. The note will have some very important information for Javad to see. Leave the mine and return to Javad in Chainscrape.

At this point, this side quest will be put on hold until you are able to further investigate what happened in the cave.

The Twilight Path

Getting Started

The Twilight Path is a quest you receive in Chainscrape, the first main settlement you encounter in The Daunt. It starts when you talk to Tap to Reveal in the tavern.

When Aloy first enters Chainscrape, she is greeted by Petra, the inventor she met in Free Heap in Horizon Zero Dawn. Petra is happy to see her old friend and invites Aloy to have a drink with her at the tavern. When Aloy arrives, the two catch up on what has happened since the Battle of the Alight. Petra tells Aloy about a group of Shadow Carja who have built a small settlement out in the mountains southwest of Chainscrape. The only problem is that they have blocked the path to valuable salvage: a large destroyed Stormbird whose heart would bring in a hefty amount of scrap. There is a person in town, Tolland, who has an interest in the heart and has threatened the Shadow Carja, now known as Twilight Carja, refugees.

Aloy agrees to talk to the settlers and convince them to leave the area.

Talk to Tolland (Optional)
Before you set out to the Twilight Carja settlement, you have the option to talk to Tolland first. His shop is located next to the Melee Pit. The conversation is less than cordial. Tolland explains that he is the rightful owner of the Stormbird heart since he was the one who knocked it down from the sky. He refuses to hear anything Aloy has to say about the refugees and is determined to confront the refugees.

Go to the Twilight Carja Camp

Make your way to the camp southwest of Chainscrape in the mountains. Once you arrive, you will hear the sounds of fighting and will see the Twilight Carja battling a group of Scroungers and Burrowers. In addition to the machines, there is also an Oseram fighting them as well, a friend of Tolland's. Defeat the Scroungers and the Burrowers and approach the camp. Aloy will meet the leader, Lokasha, and warn her about Tolland and his men. Lokasha refuses to leave because their leader, Savohar, has gone up the mountain to meditate and has been gone for three days. Worried that something might have happened to him, Aloy offers to go up the mountain to look for him.

Find Savohar

Enter the camp and go left. There will be a tall cliff you can climb that will lead to a series of ladders. Climb the ladders and follow the trail. There will be a section where you will need to use double jump, but the game will teach you how to use that ability. You will also encounter Scroungers and Burrowers, and it will be up to you to either fight them or sneak past them.

Aloy will see blood on the trail and assume it's Savohar's. Use Aloy's Focus to highlight his path, and follow it. This will take you up and around the mountain. Eventually, you will come to the end of the trail, and there you will find an injured Savohar.

Aloy talks to Savohar who looks weak and frail. Despite his serious injury, he has been meditating in the hopes that the downed Stormbird will offer him a sign of a new place for his people to call home. Aloy tries to help him, but he refuses her aid, stating that he must help his people. Aloy decides to leave him there and go seek out the Stormbird heart. If she can't help him, then the least she can do is get the heart and offer it to his people.

Get the Stormbird Heart

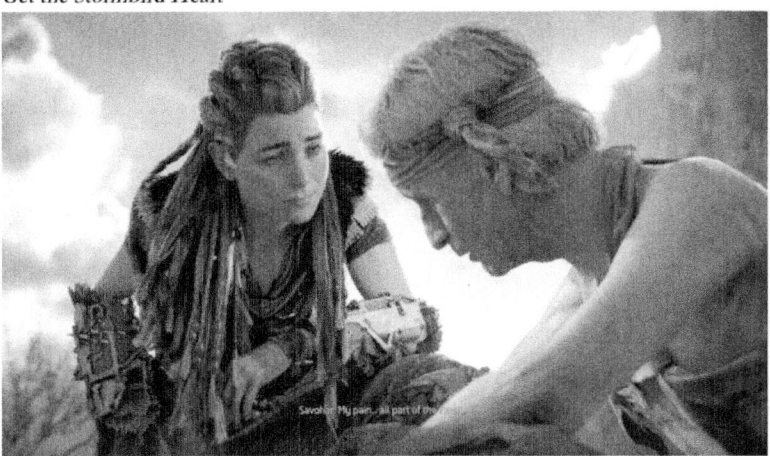

Before Savohar is a gap in the trail. Jump the gap and hang on to the side of the mountain. Climb the mountain and make your way to the tower where the Stormbird is. The climb is easy, but make sure to use your focus to highlight the yellow handholds on the mountain and on the tower itself. You will need to climb right around the tower in order to reach the top.

Once you reach the top, take the heart, take the strange lens, and open up any caches you find. Rappel down the tower and get back to Savohar.

Unfortunately, once you reach Savohar, you find that he has already passed.

Defend the Twilight Carja

You will not need to retrace your steps as there is an area to the left of Savohar that will allow you to rappel back down to the camp. As soon as you land on the ground, you will hear Tolland and his men talking to Lokasha.

When you enter the conversation, it will activate a Flashpoint. You can respond in one of three ways: logically, aggressively, or compassionately. An aggressive response will lead to a fight between Aloy and Tolland's men. A compassionate response will convince Tolland to leave the Twilight Carja alone.

After confronting Tolland, Aloy will tell Lokasha of Savohar's fate and she will give Lokasha the heart. Aloy sends them on their way to Chainscrape where Petra will look after them.

Shadow from the Past
Getting Started
Shadow from the Past is the first quest you receive in Barren Light and is the first part of a two-part questline. You can start this either before or after the events of The Embassy. In this quest, a familiar group will make their return and Aloy must do what she can to save an innocent man.

Now that The Daunt has been cleared of Bristlebacks, the Embassy can now begin. When Aloy enters the main building in Barren Light, go left and up the ramp. You will see a prisoner behind bars and a guard. Speak to the prisoner, Conover.

Speak to Conover

Conover tells Aloy about why he is behind bars. He followed a fellow guard to a place to the east of Barren Light and overheard the guard talking to someone about Eclipse. In an attempt to get closer to the conversation, Conover was discovered and had to fight for his life. Unfortunately, Conover had to kill the guard and fight off an Eclipse man in order to escape. The guards caught him and arrested him for murder. He now awaits his execution.

Upon hearing this, Aloy asks for more information about the Eclipse, but the guard doesn't believe that Eclipse has returned. Aloy is not so sure and agrees to help Conover by traveling East and investigating the site of the fight. If she can prove there was another person there, she can save Conover's life.

Head East and Follow the Tracks

After speaking with Conover head east across the river. There will be a building and a small clearing. Aloy will spot a pool of blood on the ground; the spot where Conover fought the other guard. Moving towards the mountainside, you will find some broken branches, a clue that perhaps someone else was there. Follow the trail up the mountain. Along the way, Aloy will see additional spots of blood on the ground. Using the focus, highlight the bloodstains and follow the footprints across a bridge. Underneath the bridge will be a small makeshift campsite: the place where the injured Eclipse man tended to his wounds.

Use the focus again to highlight the path the person made and follow it. Eventually, you will find a cave.

Enter the Cave and Kill the Eclipse

Upon entering the cave, you will hear some voices. Going further in will reveal a small patrol of Eclipse men. Some of them are talking about the new Eclipse leader, Vezreh.

You can either stealthily and kill the Eclipse or you can go in and cause a big commotion. Either way, you must take out the Eclipse guards and clear the cave. Exit the cave through the opening on the left and continue forward towards the Eclipse hideout.

Search Rayad's Corpse

The Eclipse hideout will not be far but you will have to climb the side of a mountain to get there. Once you are in, you will see Rayad's corpse covered and laying on the floor. This was the Eclipse member that Conover fought. Search his body and you will find a note about Eclipse's plans to infiltrate Barren Light and more information about Vezreh. It is all you need to prove that Rayad was a part of Eclipse and that Conover had saved many lives by doing what he did.

ERRANDS

This Horizon Forbidden West Errand Quest (or Errands) guide is your handy tool for locating and completing all the errands in the game. This guide will walk you through each errand and will give you information about the recommended level, location of the errands, and the rewards.

There are two ways to get an Errand Quest: going into a settlement and following the bright green exclamation point on the map or listening to a rumor (marked on the map with a bright green exclamation point inside a bright green circle). Because of this, there is no way to distinguish between a Side Quest and an Errand until you accept the quest and it's added to your log.

Horizon Forbidden West includes Tap to Reveal. Errands are given to you by people in need of assistance in a variety of tasks such as fetching items, finding people, or gathering resources. Most Errands are not as long as Side Quests, so expect to spend about 30 minutes to complete an Errand. Errands also do not reward as much experience and skill points as Side Quests, but you can still earn unique weapons, armor, and face paints.

A Bigger Boom
Talk to Delah and Boomer

While walking around Chainscrape, Aloy overhears two sisters talking nearby the southwest exit of town. It sounds like they need some assistance in gathering materials. Aloy stops by to ask them what they need. Delah explains that her sister Boomer is trying to craft a new weapon. The only problem is that they don't have all the parts they need. Aloy offers to gather the materials for them.

You will need to collect 3 Charger Horn and 1 Fanghorn Rib. If you activate the quest, it will mark on your map where to find a nearby Charger site, as well as the specific Fanghorn you need a rib from.

How to Get Charger Horns

The Chargers have a site near Chainscrape that you can visit, marked on your map. Chargers are not very strong machines, but they have a bucking attack that can do some damage if you're too close. Keep dodging the Chargers while shooting at their horns with non-elemental ammo. This is the only way to ensure you get the components you need.

How to Get a Fanghorn Rib

As for the Fanghorn Rib, you will need to go to an area east of the Charger site to find the specific Fire Fanghorn you need. Unlike other Fanghorns, this one has powerful fire attacks. You don't need to target any specific parts to get the Rib, as it's a special part attached to this quest Fanghorn.

Deliver the Parts to Get A New Weapon

Once you have gathered the components, return to Delah at Chainscrape. She will give the parts to Boomer and she will craft the Tap to Reveal. As a token of their appreciation, they let Aloy keep the weapon.

A Dash of Courage

Getting Started

A cook in the Chainscape needs supplies and ingredients in order to keep the people fed. In doing so Aloy will learn about the power of a well-cooked meal.

Upon entering the Tavern in Chainscape, Aloy hears the cook, Milduf, complaining about needing some ingredients to keep up with the demand of his customers. Aloy stops by to talk to Milduf and learns that he does not have everything he needs. Aloy offers to go out into the wild to pick up supplies for him.

Wild Meat and Bitter Leaf

Mildruf asks Aloy to collect 5 Wild Meat and 3 Bitter Leaf. These items can be found around Chainscape. The Wild Meat comes from hunting wild animals like boar. The bitter leaf grows on rocky terrain, so the mountains to the west of Chainscape are the best place to look. Mildruf will also ask for a corrugated metal panel. This can only be found at a Scrounger site in one of their many scrap piles.

Go to the Scrounger Site

Head to the Scrounger site once you get the Wild Meat and Bitter Leaf. There will be a few Scroungers that you will have to defeat. Scroungers are weak against Frost and Acid damage and they are not strong against any elemental attacks. They do have shock attacks but they charge up before firing it. Ranged attacks work best as they have some useful components on their back.

Now that they are out of your way, you can search the scrap piles for the metal panel Mildruf needs.

Return to Mildruf

Now that you have all the items, return to Mildruf. He will be very appreciative and offer to cook Aloy a meal. She will try to refuse, but his instance pays off. The meal will give Aloy a health bonus that will last for a time.

COLLECTIBLES

Relic Ruin Ornaments

Relic Ruins are specific ruins left by the Old Ones, and act as dungeon-like puzzle levels. They're a great way to get XP and Skill Points because they never feature combat, just puzzle solving. At the end of each one is a mysterious Ornament, which Aloy doesn't initially know the function of.

Ornaments are the spherical Orbs you find at the end of a Relic Ruin, and appear to be themed after a holiday celebrated by the Old Ones. When she first finds them, Aloy doesn't have any clue what to do with them, but keeps them anyway just in case.

Relic Ruin: The Daunt

The first Relic Ruin in the game is found in The Daunt, the opening valley of the game proper. It'll be found South of Chainscrape, East of Redhew Quarry, and very close to The Daunt's Vista Point.

Quest Stats

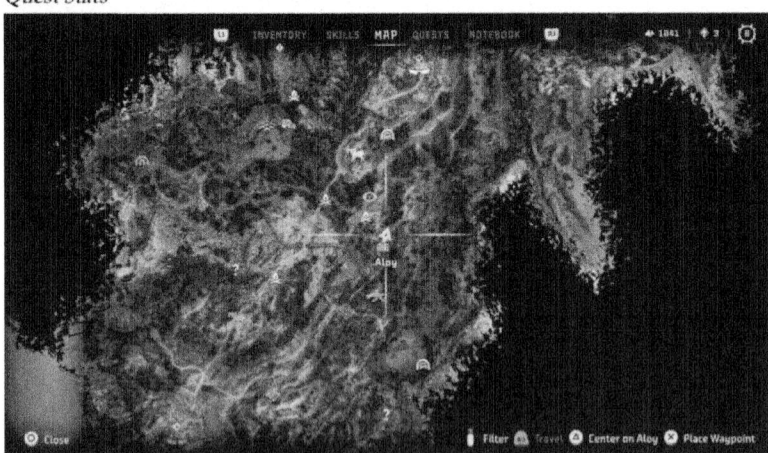

Treasures await those who dare explore the ruins of the Old World.

Location: The Daunt

XP: Tap to Reveal

Skill Points: Tap to Reveal

How to Complete The Daunt Relic Ruin

The Relic Ruins in The Daunt are found directly South of Chainscrape and East of the quarry. It's also the subject of the nearby Vista Point between it and the quarry. There's a Campfire close to it you can use to fast travel if you found it.

The starting point is the Northern end of the ruins, where the Crate is.

Head inside, then look up for a handhold on the upper floor. Drag the Crate in here and use it to get up.

On the upper floor, you'll notice a locked door, which is only unlocked via a Key Module Terminal to the left of it. In addition to this you'll need a passcode to use once the Key is inside.

Exit onto the nearby balcony, then Sprint and run up the ramp so you make the jump across to the other side.

Drop down through the doorway, and you'll land in a clearing. A Datapoint will be visible on the bench in front of you: highlight it with your Focus, then press the Touchpad to bring up its Notebook entry. Reading it, you'll learn that the passcode for the door is Tap to Reveal.

First though you need to get to the next section of the ruin. Facing the Datapoint, look up and to your right to spot two blue grates, one on a vent cover, and another on a metal beam. Pull them with the Pullcaster to open the vent and lower the beam to get up there.

Ancient Supply Chest - Look on the small wall segment directly above the Datapoint to spot this sitting on top: pull it down with your Pullcaster.

To reach the vent, look at the opposite side of the room to see a Crate: pull it down with the Pullcaster and move it into position.

With the Crate in place, jump up onto the beam and then onto the vent cover, then crawl through to the next room.

The room will have practically nothing in it, just a big hole on the left side. That said...

Ancient Supply Box - At the back of the room, behind the hole in the floor.

Jump into the hole in the floor to make it to the basement. You'll see a ledge you can use on the back wall, but as soon as you jump on, it'll collapse. You'll have to improvise a way up to the other handholds here.

To start, turn around and head into the dark area of the basement. While this looks like a dead-end, if you look up you can spot a blue grate you can tug with the Pullcaster to make a hole in the floor.

Next, head back up and look for the wall with the blue grate on it: pull this down to reveal not just the hole in the floor you made earlier, but also the Crate you used to get into the vent!

Push the Crate into the hole in the floor to drop it down into the basement, then push it up to the base of the wall where the collapsed ledge is.

Now jump onto the Crate and climb up onto the roof using the provided handholds.

Ancient Supply Box - Sitting on the roof after you get up using the handholds.

Now look down over the Western edge of the building to spot a wooden balcony. Jump down to it!

On the balcony you can find a Key Module for the hotel room, which will have a white icon hovering above it. Pick it up, you'll need it to get through the locked door!

Ancient Supply Box - At the far end of the balcony, close to the next handholds.

Use the yellow handholds close to the Ancient Supply Box listed above to get onto the roof. Carefully navigate around it to get back to the very first room in whatever manner you please (avoid falling into the second room, because the only way out of there is through the basement and back onto the roof again).

The Daunt Relic Ruin Passcode Solution

Once you're back at the locked door, use the Key Module Terminal to insert the key. Then, input the passcode:

The Daunt Relic Ruin Passcode: Tap to Reveal

The door will unlock and you can head inside! Pick up the Ornament, and...

Ancient Supply Safe - Behind the locked door, to the left of the Ornament.

Vista Points
How Vista Points Work

Vista Points have become a tad more complex since Zero Dawn. First, you'll need to locate an Old Ones satellite tower, then scan it with the Focus. This gives you a clue for what the subject of the Vista is, in the form of a fragmented picture, and a Search Zone will appear on your map when you Activate the landmark.

The subject of the Vista is always a Relic Ruin of the Old Ones, marked on the map with an icon of ruined buildings. The challenge is to line up the Focus' view so that it matches the picture fragment clue you were given. Study the Relic Ruin so that you can match up basic shapes with the picture; if these details are smaller in the picture, you'll need to be further away.

When you think you're in the right spot, activate the Focus and look at the Relic Ruin: if you're in the right spot, the full color picture will reveal itself, and you'll unlock some lore in the Collectibles section of your Notebook!

Vista Point: The Daunt
The Vista Point Tower in The Daunt is located just South of Chainscrape; look for a satellite tower between two Campfires, just South of a Charger Mount Site. The location of the vista itself is at the base of a ruined bridge on the riverbank, just a tad North of the Tower itself.

Signal Lenses
Lens of Dawn
How to Get the Lens of Dawn

As noted above, the Lens of Dawn is located in the Northern end of The Daunt. Specifically it's found just East of a Shelter across the river, and North of a Charger Mount Site.

Start by going to the base of the cliff the tower is on and looking for the wooden platforms at its base. It's here that you can start your climb up the cliffs. Remember that if you're having trouble knowing where to go, you can pulse your Focus to reveal handholds, or turn them on permanently in the Visual Settings.

As you climb, you'll want to make sure you veer to the right and around the corner. This will put you in reach of a series of Grapple Points, letting you use your Pullcaster to speed up your ascent of the cliffs.

After the third Grapple Point, you'll be climbing the tower itself; climb up the yellow wooden beams to start the path on the way up. Make sure to check the room you start in, and around the corner of the balcony, for chests with some loot in them.

When you get to the top, there'll be a large brass reflector dish. The Lens of Dawn will be on the end of the wooden arm of the dish.

Once you have it, use the pair of Rappel beams to get down to the starting platforms!

Lens of Morning
How to Get the Lens of Morning

As noted above, the Lens of Morning is located in the Northern part of The Daunt, on the cliffs North-East of Chainscrape.

To start climbing it, look for some old wooden platforms at the base of the cliff it's on to start from. Remember to use Climbing Annotations with your Focus to see the way forward.

When you get to the top, loot the chest, then climb up the ladder to make it onto a balcony. It'll have a Metal Flower on it extending vines over a small part of the tower. You unfortunately cannot remove it without an item acquired later in the game.

Climb through one of the windows and make your way clockwise around the tower. When you walk down the yellow beams, head around the corner, drop the ladder, then go around the next corner. Here, look up to spot a Grapple Point high above to speed up the climb.

Here, head around the left corner for another chest, then go around the next corner and climb up the handholds to reach the top of the tower. The Signal Lens will be on the wooden arm extending out of the brass dish.

Once you have it, use the pair of Rappel beams to get down to the starting platforms!

Lens of Midday
How to Get the Lens of Midday

The Lens of Midday, as noted above, is in the middle portion of The Daunt, specifically up the cliffs to the East of Chainscrape. You can get there by using the bridge going East of Chainscrape.

As always, look for some wooden structures that mark where to begin the climb. Its a rather complicated ascent, so make sure to use Climbing Annotations with either the Focus or the Visual Settings.

As you approach the top, you'll have to jump across a large gap, climb a cliff, then jump again to the top of a rock pillar. From here you need to turn right and climb along the cliff face to get to the next area, but without the Climbing Annotations, this isn't very obvious.

When you get to the top of the cliffs, head left to find a chest to loot, then start your ascent by going anti-clockwise around the corners of the tower. The path will have you double-back and go clockwise, however.

When you reach the top, the Signal Lens will be on the end of the wooden arm sticking out of the copper dish.

Once you have it, use the four Rappel beams to get down to the starting platforms (although only three of them are strictly required).

Lens of Afternoon
How to Get the Lens of Afternoon

The Lens of Afternoon is unique because it's the only lens that's locked behind a Side Quest. In this case, you'll need to start "The Twilight Path" Side Quest in order to access the path up.

The Twilight Path will in fact lead you all the way up to the top of the tower, so for detailed instructions, visit that page of our guide.

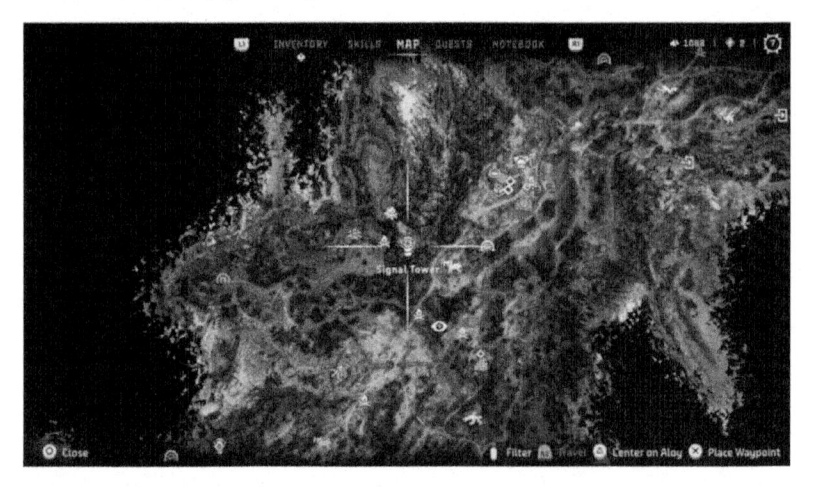

When you get to the top, there won't be the usual brass reflector dish, since it was destroyed by the Stormbird. However you can see the dish's wooden arm sticking out of some rubble in a rooftop's corner, where you can simply pick it up.

The way down is also done as in The Twilight Path. Jump across the broken bridge, then head for the Carja lookout on the far left and Rappel down to the bottom.

Lens of Twilight
How to Get the Lens of Twilight

The Lens of Twilight, as noted above, is found in the Southern section of The Daunt, specifically up the cliffs directly East of Barren Light and the local Hunting Grounds.

Unlike all the other Signal Lenses, however, the Lens of Twilight isn't reached by climbing straight up the cliff face. Instead, you have to follow the road leading up the South of it, and climb up from there. This ascent is relatively straight-forward, but can be sped up if you can chain the two Grapple Points together.

At the top, you'll walk through an abandoned camp on the way to the tower. You can find a chest to loot here, and a second one in the shrubs at the base of the tower.

Check the left side of the tower for a blue grate on the wall, which you can yank with the Pullcaster to make a hole in the wall. Through here you can start going clockwise around the tower to ascend it.

When you reach the very top of the tower, the Lens of Twilight will be on the end of the wooden arm on the brass dish.

Once you have it, use the pair of Rappel beams to get down to the starting platforms!

Lens of Evening
How to Get the Lens of Evening

As noted above, the Lens of Evening is located in the Southern area of The Daunt, and is directly North of Barren Light. It's part of the "Signals of the Sun" Errand Quest, so for detailed instructions on how to get up there, visit that page of our guide.

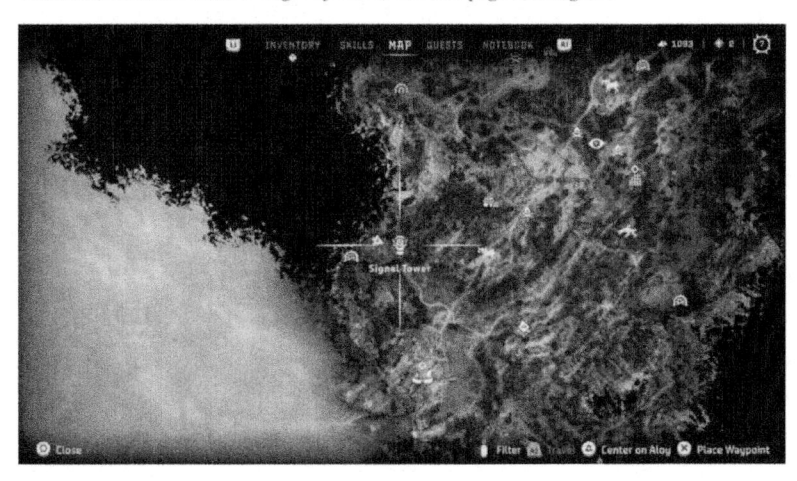

Once you've recovered the lens, you should look for Raynah so that you can hand the Lens in to her. You only need to return the Lens of Evening to complete the quest, however you'll get more rewards if you can give her the other five lenses. Giving Raynah the Lense of Evening will also mark the locations of all remaining lenses on the map!

CHARACTERS AND VOICE ACTORS

When you join Aloy on her next great journey in Horizon Forbidden West you'll encounter a variety of characters, both old and new. Whether you need a refresher on Forbidden West's returning figures or you need help pinpointing who's behind one of the new voices added to Horizon Zero Dawn's already star-studded cast, this guide has everything you need to know.

Continue reading or click on any of the links below to learn more about the corresponding characters and their voice actors:

Aloy

Aloy is Horizon Forbidden West's fearless and warmhearted protagonist. Once an outcast, Aloy has become the greatest machine hunter in the world of Horizon. Tap to Reveal, Aloy is now on a quest to uncover the secrets hidden in the Forbidden West so she can rid the world of the blight before it's too late.

How Old is Aloy?

Aloy is roughly 18-20 years old.

Born in 3021, Aloy is raised by fellow outcast and surrogate father, Rost. After her naming ceremony in the opening moments of Horizon Zero Dawn, the story jumps to "Six years later". Aloy, frustrated by the way she's shunned by the Nora tribe, takes off in a sprint and unwittingly falls into an ancient bunker.

Within this ancient bunker, Aloy discovers her Focus.

Later, we're treated to a training montage where Rost prepares Aloy to win the Proving. As the montage comes to a close we experience another 12-year time leap meaning that Aloy was roughly 18 years old during the events of Horizon Zero Dawn.

In Horizon Forbidden West, Aloy and several other characters make reference to a 6-month time gap since the conclusion of Zero Dawn which allows us to safely determine that Aloy may be as young as 18 but no older than 20 years old.

Aloy's Voice Actor - Ashly Burch

Reprising her role as Aloy is one of the most renowned voice actors in video games, Ashly Burch. In addition to her roles in TV series such as Mythic Quest and Final Space, Burch is highly regarded for her work as Tiny Tina in the Borderlands series, Viper in Valorant, Chloe Price in Life is Strange, Mel in The Last of Us: Part II, and many more.

Sylens

Aloy's frenemy, the enigmatic and self-serving Sylens is back for Horizon Forbidden West. Sylens was last seen in Horizon Zero Dawn's conclusion Tap to Reveal

Sylens Voice Actor - Lance Reddick

Returning to the role of Sylens is prolific actor Lance Reddick. If you recognize Sylens' voice or likeness you've likely seen or heard Reddick in roles such as Commander Zavala (Destiny franchise), Charon (John Wick franchise), or Cedric Daniels from The Wire.

Erend

One of Aloy's earliest allies, Erend, also makes a return in Horizon's sequel. The leader of the Oseram tribe's Vanguard, Erend will support Aloy along her journey to stop the blight.

Erend Voice Actor - John Hopkins

Erend is voiced by John Hopkins who is known for portraying Erik Ahlberg in Netflix's Hilda and Lucas Grey in IO Interactive's Hitman franchise.

Varl

After swearing an oath to help Aloy, the Nora Brave Varl from Horizon Zero Dawn will have a larger presence in Forbidden West.

Varl Voice Actor - John Macmillan

In addition to having roles in other video games such as Amnesia: Rebirth, John Macmillan will be playing Ser Laenor Velaryon in HBO's upcoming Game of Thrones spinoff series, House of the Dragon.

Regalla

One of the most notable newcomers to Horizon Forbidden West is Regalla. Little is known about the rebel leader except Tap to Reveal

Regalla Voice Actor

Regalla is voiced by the incomparable Tap to Reveal

Tilda

Tilda is undoubtedly the most mysterious addition to the Horizon cast and it's said that she has a "special connection to the ancient past".

Tilda Voice Actor

Tilda is voiced by the distinguished Tap to Reveal

Additional Characters and Voice Actors
Kotallo - Noshir Dalal

"Raised by the Tenakth Sky Clan, Kotallo is a stoic and imposing warrior. As a young soldier, he became a Marshal – a roving lawgiver who enforces the peace that the tribe's leader, Hekarro, has established". [1]

Voice actor Noshir Dalal is also known for playing:

Charles Smith - Red Dead Redemption II

Khalil - Call of Duty: Black Ops II

Various Roles - Star Wars: The Bad Batch

Zo - Erica Luttrell

"Zo hails from the agrarian tribe of the Utaru. She has devoted herself to providing care and comfort to her people as a Gravesinger – one who helps the ailing make a peaceful transition into death". [1]

Voice actor Erica Luttrell is also known for playing:

Shuri - Marvel's Avengers DLC

Sapphire - Steven Universe

New Mother - Westworld

Alva - Alison Jaye

"Alva is a member of a mysterious new tribe that Aloy encounters in the Forbidden West. Curious and brilliant but unsure of herself, her job is to help her people interpret the ancient past". [1]

Voice actor Alison Jaye is also known for playing:

Julia Nicolo - Shameless

Nicole - Unbelievable

Sandra - Call Jane

GAIA - Lesley Ewen

"GAIA is the central governing intelligence of the Zero Dawn terraforming system, responsible for bringing life back to a barren Earth after its destruction a thousand years ago. As told in Horizon Zero Dawn, she Tap to Reveal She'll be making a return in Horizon Forbidden West to help Aloy stop the blight and save humankind". [1]

ABOUT THE AUTHOR

I When I finding new tricks, tips, and strategies to beat each other, they came up with a brilliant idea. Let's take these hours of gaming expertise, and share these skills with like mind people. At that moment, the Horizon Forbidden West Complete Guide & Walkthrough were born. With more exciting gaming books being developed in the Lab as we speak. I am creating a buzz in the gaming guide publishing world, with a ground swell of followers, anxiously awaiting my new releases.

Printed in Great Britain
by Amazon